The Encyclopedia of

Motorcycles

Hongdu–Moto Guzzi

The *Encyclopedia of* Motorcycles

Hongdu–Moto Guzzi

Peter Henshaw

Chelsea House Publishers
Philadelphia

Published in 2000 by
Chelsea House Publishers
1974 Sproul Road, Suite 400
P.O. Box 914
Broomall. PA 19008-0914

ISBN 0-7910-6055-1

Printed in Singapore

Library of Congress Cataloging-in-Publication Data applied for

ABOVE: Hongdu HD125

HONGDU *China 1965–*
A licence-built Yamaha YG1. Still builds Yamaha-based lightweights.

HOOCK *Germany 1926–28*
The German Villiers importer also fitted the 342cc (21cu in) unit to some of its own frames.

HOREX *Germany 1923–60*
Diversification for a glassware manufacturer. The first bikes used Oberursel engines of 250–600cc (15–37cu in) but were not a huge success, so Horex began to build Sturmey-Archer engines under licence, and went on to design its own power units, all sold under the Colombus name. There were a great variety on offer, the most famous being the large, technically advanced ohc vertical twins of 1932, which grew up to 980cc

RIGHT and OPPOSITE: A 1951 Horex 400cc (24cu in) with Steib sidecar

(60cu in) and saw competition success. Production restarted in 1948 with a 350 single, though 250 singles and a 500 twin were soon added, plus a scooter and a 98cc (6cu in) lightweight. Production ceased in 1960, though there was an attempt at a relaunch in 1980 with Sachs-engined mopeds which was short-lived.

HORSY *France 1952–53*
An 83cc (5cu in) two-stroke scooter.

HOSK *Japan 1953–57*
A complete range, from 123cc (7.5cu in) two-strokes to 498cc (30cu in) four-strokes (similar to Horex) twins.

HOSKINSON *England 1919–22*
Step-through frames and choice of three engines (Villiers, Union, Blackburne) of similar sizes.

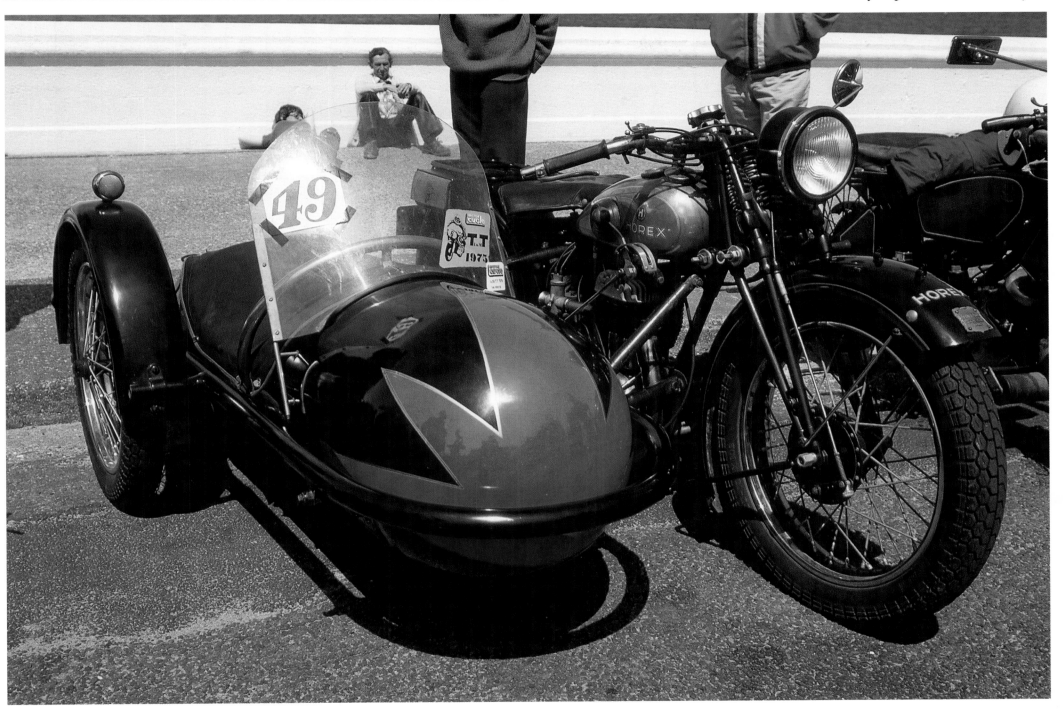

HOWARD *England 1905–07*
A pioneering attempt at fuel injection with a 2.5hp single.

H&R *Germany 1921–25*
Forerunner of Heros, with its own 155–249cc (9.5–15cu in) sv engines.

H&R (R&H) *England 1922–25*
147cc (9cu in) Villiers-engined two-strokes. The H&R stood for Hailstone and Ravenhall, which sometimes (blood on the boardroom carpet?) became Ravenhall and Hailstone.

HRD *England 1927–55*
See Vincent-HRD.

HT *England 1920–22*
Another attempt at a car-like motorcycle, with enclosed engines and leaf-sprung rear-end. First produced machines with 292cc (18cu in) Union two-strokes, then 346cc (21cu in) Barr & Strouds.

HUC *Germany 1924–25*
Used 145/172cc (9/10.5cu in) DKW engines.

HUFFER *Germany 1923–25*
Used a variety of engines for these up-to-198cc (12cu in) lightweights.

HULBERT-BRAMLEY *England 1903–06*
Built lightweights and the Binks-designed 385cc (23.5cu in) four-cylinder machines.

HULLA *Germany 1925–32*
Mainly DKW-powered two-strokes of 173–298cc (11–18cu in) in its own frames.

HULSMANN *The Netherlands 1939–55*
Used exclusively Villiers engines of 123–225cc (7.5–14cu in).

HUMBER *England 1896–1930*
Humber's involvement in motorcycles was a relatively sporadic one, even though it was spread over 34 years. Thomas Humber had begun making bicycles in the 1870s, but exhibited a number of solo and tandem motorized cycles at the International Horseless Carriage Exhibition in May 1896. It wasn't until 1902 that Humber Ltd. began selling motorcycles, and then it was a 2hp machine built under licence from Phelon & Moore (*see* Panther). Variations on the theme followed, but after three years the range was dropped.

Humber's next was a 3.5hp machine of its own design, announced in 1909, with the advanced feature of sprung front forks. It was joined in 1910 by a smaller 2hp single, a year which also saw a works team entered for the TT and P.J. Evans winning the Junior for Humber. A Tourist Trophy model joined the catalogue soon after, proving that there is nothing new about the race replicas. Meanwhile, bikes were getting bigger, and Humber responded with a decidedly odd three-cylinder 6hp designed for sidecar work. The three cylinders were horizontally opposed, with one large one (78mm x 78mm) facing forwards, and a smaller twin (55mm x 78mm) to the rear. Few were made.

A seed of an idea must have taken root, however, as flat twins soon became a staple part of the Humber range, with both air- and water-cooled 6hp versions offered until civilian production ceased during World War I. Production restarted in 1919, and the

ABOVE: Humber 341cc (21cu in)

following year saw an updated 600cc 4.5hp version of the air-cooled twin, now with chain-drive and a three-speed gearbox. A 349cc (21cu in) single joined the range in 1923, which did well in the Six Days Trial that year, and when the twin was phased out became Humber's sole motorcycle offering. It acquired an overhead-valve engine in 1927, and in 1928 a bevel-drive overhead-cam version appeared. Like Velocette, the Humbers were quality machines which cost more than a BSA or Ariel, for example, but unlike Velocette, Humber no longer had the racing success to back it up. The Rootes company was taking increasing control of Humber, and motorcycles did not feature in its plans. The Humber 350s were dropped in 1930.

HÜMMEL Germany 1951–54
Best known for the 120–149cc (7–9cu in) Sitta scooters, but produced lightweights as well. All were Ilo-powered.

HUNWICK HALLAM Australia 1999–
Australia is known for many things, but until recently motorcycling wasn't one of them, hence the surprise worldwide when the Hunwick Hallam V-twin was revealed in October 1996. It was the result of a partnership between Australia's largest bike dealer, Rod Hunwick, and the race-bike tuner Paul Hallam. They proposed an all-new, all-Australian range of 90-degree one-litre V-twins, which would include the X1R, a new contender for World Superbike racing.

Much was made of the X1R at the original launch, as much for its proposed use of pneumatic valves as anything else, and the partners confirmed it to be part of a range which would include a 1350cc (82cu in) muscle bike named the Power

Cruiser, and a 1150cc (70cu in) version, the Rage sports roadster. By early 1999 the X1R had already raced successfully (ridden by Honda rider Mal Campbell) and the Rage was undergoing final homologation tests, on target for production in the following June. What with Hunwick Hallam, Voxan, Excelsior-Henderson and Victory, 1999 seems a good year for all-new motorcycle marques.

HURIKAN Czechoslovakia 1947–49
An advanced 247cc (15cu in) ohc single sportster, though few were made.

HURTU France 1906–58
Intermittent production, but produced mostly 49cc (3cu in) mopeds after 1945.

HUSAR Germany 1923–25
269cc (16cu in) sv singles with leaf-sprung rear suspension on all models.

HUSQVARNA Sweden 1903–
Began using Moto-Rêve, NSU and FN engines, and in fact didn't produce its own engine (a 550cc/34cu inch sv V-twin) until 1920. Continued to buy in singles, however, notably from Sturmey-Archer and JAP, while the V-twin grew to a 992cc (60cu in) version with 22hp. But Husqvarna's most famous inter-war model was a racer, the new ohv V-twin of 1932. Designed by Folke Mannerstedt and Calle Heimdahl, the 498cc (30cu in) twin was a new challenge to racing dominated by single-cylinder machines. Development pushed the power up to 36hp, while weight was cut to 125kg (276lb) and a 348cc (21cu in) version was developed as well. It managed three successive victories in the Swedish GP, and

ABOVE: Husqvarna 250cc (15cu in) motocrosser

BELOW: Husqvarna 250cc road bike

Stanley Woods broke the lap record on one during the 1934 TT. Husqvarna built its first two-stroke (a basic 98cc/6cu inch two-speeder) in 1935, and after the war was to concentrate most of its attention on two-strokes. It also focused increasingly on off-road competition, and was rewarded with great success with ten World Motocross titles between 1960 and 1970. Four-stroke off-roaders were reintroduced in the 1980s, and in 1986 the company was taken over by the rapidly growing Cagiva group. Production was transferred to Italy the following year, where the Husqvarna range has continued to develop, an example being the 577cc (35cu in) TC610 of 1992, with a 50bhp water-cooled four-valve dohc single, six-speed gearbox and high quality suspension. In 1998, with the market for supermotos in full swing, Husqvarna announced a return to the road market with the TE610, a slightly more civilized TC with road tyres and electric start.

HUY *Germany 1923–26*
198cc (12cu in) sv singles, followed by 347cc (21cu in) MAG-engined machines.

I

IBIS *Italy 1925–28*
Piazza 173cc (11cu in) engine in a step-through frame.

IDEAL *Germany 1924–25*
Used own 173cc (11cu in) three-port two-stroke engine.

IDEAL-JAWA *India 1960–80*
A Jawa-based 250cc (15cu in) two-stroke single, still in production under the Monarch and Road King names.

IDRA *Italy 1923–25*
A 123cc (7.5cu in) ohv single, available as a clip-on or as a complete lightweight bike.

IDROFLEX *Italy 1949–54*
A 105cc (6cu in) two-stroke engine was mounted on the swinging arm.

IFA *East Germany 1945–60*
See MZ.

ILO *Germany 1923–25*
Built two-stroke singles of 117–170cc (7–10cu in), and supplied countless small German assemblers with ready-made power units. Ilo built its own machines for a couple of years, but demand for its engines soon put a stop to that.

IMHOLZ *Switzerland 1924–27*
Own 123/173cc (7.5/11cu in) two-strokes, and a Moser-powered ohv 173cc.

IMME *Germany 1948–51*
An unusual 148cc (9cu in) two-stroke whose power unit swung with rear-wheel movement. The exhaust pipe formed part of the frame and there was a single-sided front fork.

IMN *Italy 1950–58*
The Naples-based firm first built 49–248cc (3–15cu in) two-strokes, but lost its way with an underdeveloped 198cc (12cu in) flat twin which was enough to bring down the company.

IMPERIA *Germany 1923–25*
Assembled 346 and 496cc (21 and 30cu in) JAP engines in step-through frames.

The Imperial, a very early American V-twin

IMPERIA *Germany 1924–35*
No connection with the above, it started off using mainly MAG power units, most of which were V-twins. Collapsed after a couple of years, but was bought by the Schrödter family in 1926. At first, the new owners continued the buy-in philosophy, from MAG, JAP and Python, but new boss Rolf Schrödter designed an unorthodox double-pistoned supercharged single and a flat-twin two-stroke. It was all too ambitious for Imperia's limited resources and the company closed.

IMPERIAL *England 1901–04*
Used 3.5hp Coronet engines, with atmospheric inlet valves.

IMPERIAL *U.S.A. 1903–c.1910*
A 444cc (27cu in) single-cylinder machine.

INDIAN *U.S.A. 1901–53*
Only one manufacturer seriously challenged Harley-Davidson's bid for domination of the American motorcycle market – Indian. In fact, the Wigwam, as it was known, was a couple of years ahead of Harley's offering right from the start, and in Indian's peak year of 1913 (when it built nearly 32,000 bikes) could claim to be the largest manufacturer in the world. But within a couple of decades it was well and truly the runner-up, and only survived another few years after World War II. It all came down to ownership: in that same record year of 1913, control of Indian passed from the two enthusiasts who established it, to shareholders whose main priority was neither design, nor the long-term health of the company, but profits. Harley-Davidson, on the other hand, was owned and controlled by the same two families right up until the late 1960s. Continuity of leadership counts for a lot, as Indian was to find to its cost.

All this was in the future when George Hendee and Oscar Hedström met at a cycle race in 1900. It was to be the perfect combination: Hendee was the businessman, Hedström the slightly younger engineer, and both these keen cyclists wished to get into the motorized

1915 was the year Indian offered an electric-start option. However, there were few takers

bicycle business. But they had a different approach to Bill Harley and the Davidsons who had proceeded with rather more caution and sold their early machines by word of mouth. Instead, the two signed a contract to produce 'a motor-driven bicycle that could be produced in volume' and Hedström built the first 213cc (13cu in) prototype in less than five months. It was then demonstrated in front of public, press and potential investors and there was a national advertising campaign. From the start, Indian appeared to be a serious business proposition.

It had a good basis in Oscar Hedström's first prototype, for the Swedish-born engineer incorporated such advanced features as chain-drive (when everyone else relied on the likely to slip belt-drive) and his motor proved tractable and reliable. Money was duly raised and production began in Hendee's bicycle factory in Springfield, Massachusetts. Production soared: from 143 bikes in 1902, to 376 the following year, then to nearly 600, then to approaching 1,200 by 1905 in comparison to Harley who built just 16 machines that year. The Indian single soon became a familiar sight in hillclimbs, endurance runs and beach racing, either ridden by Hedström himself or a gifted young rider named Jacob DeRosier.

Nor was the design laying stagnant: a twist-grip throttle was added in 1905 (actually pioneered by Glenn Curtiss), a spring fork featured on the road bikes and in 1907 Indian unveiled its first road-going V-twin. It was rated at 4 horsepower and was of 640cc (39cu in), with a side exhaust valve and overhead atmospheric inlet valve. Its 42-degree cylinder angle (like Harley's

A 1906 Indian. At this time, the company had a headstart on Harley-Davidson

45) was to become an Indian trademark. It was at about this time that Indian began to build its engine in-house, where it had previously been contracted out to Aurora.

In 1908 (with production now at over 3,000) the single and V-twin racers received mechanical inlet valves, which appeared on the road bikes the following

year. Loop frames were another new feature, signifying a final break with the bicycle-style diamond frame. It was in fact a period of innovation, particularly for American manufacturers, and 1910 saw the leaf-sprung front fork and a two-speed transmission, plus a clutch for the single-speed direct-drive single. The following

year, four valves per cylinder arrived, with the 8-valve V-twin racer which won a whole string of speed records and was usually ridden by Jacob DeRosier. This was also the year of Indian's historic 1-2-3 placing in the Isle of Man TT. Indian's star rider actually finished 12th that time, being unused to inferior European roads, but

A 1912 V-twin, produced when Indian was at its peak

made up for it the following week at Brooklands by beating Charlie Collier of Matchless.

End of an Era

Meanwhile, with demand and production ever increasing (nearly 20,000 machines were built in 1911, which produced profits

of half a million dollars), Hendee was initiating ambitious plans for growth, with new plant and machinery, and the only way to do this was to offer more shares to the public. Alarmed by the high cost of the racing and expansion programme, the new army of shareholders began to pressurize Hendee into cutting costs and increasing

profits. It was all too much for Oscar Hedström, and when his friend and protégé Jacob DeRosier died of injuries sustained in an earlier race accident, he resigned from Indian. What was in many ways Indian's golden era had passed.

One of Hedström's last jobs had been to develop an electric start for the V-twin

(another Indian innovation). He had been sceptical, but the far-sighted George Hendee had insisted that this was the route to expanding the motorcycle market, and the Hendee Special of 1914 boasted electric lights as well as starting. However, it was possibly too far ahead of its time and only lasted a year. Better news that year was

Erwin G. Baker's record-breaking run across America when he rode from San Diego to New York in $11^1/_2$ days, the first of many such records. Although electric starting had failed to find favour with the buyers, electric lighting did, and remained an option in 1915. But then George Hendee resigned from Indian and the last link with the golden era was over. Moreover, for the second year running, production and profits were down and Indian was beginning to feel the pinch of competition from Harley-Davidson and Henry Ford's Model T. Neither did Indian do well out of the war when it neglected the home market in favour of army contracts which failed to be very lucrative in any case: Harley-Davidson, however, was not slow in leaping in to fill that breach.

The year 1916 saw a replacement for the pioneering V-twin in the form of the Powerplus, a sidevalve twin that was slightly more powerful and easier to maintain. It was the work of Charles Gustafson, who had replaced Oscar Hedström, and laid the foundation for Indian's big V-twins for the future. Less successful was the little two-stroke Model K and the 257cc (16cu in) Model O, a flat twin aimed at non-enthusiasts. Both were soon dropped. It was not a happy time, and in 1919 Indian's board of directors decided to sell to a group of investors headed by a banker named Henry Skinner. Fortunately, general manager Frank Weschler was a long-term employee and remained committed to the firm, Oscar Hedström was tempted back for a short time to try to solve racing and production problems, while an Irishman named Charlie Franklin (he had been the third-placed rider in that 1911 TT)

took over the engineering side.

Matters began to improve, notably with Franklin's 600cc (37cu in) Scout V-twin of 1923, which was basically a smaller version of the Powerplus. He was quick to realize that in the new leisure motorcycle market there would be an unfulfilled demand for a middleweight bike similar to those in Europe. He was right, and the Scout was strong, fast and durable, and turned out to be a real success, the Springfield factory finding it necessary to add a second shift to cope with demand. This, in turn, made the Powerplus look a little old-fashioned, and it wasn't long before the factory responded with an enlarged Scout, the 1000cc (61cu in) Chief, a name that was to remain with Indian right to the end. It was soon followed by the 1200cc (73cu in) Big Chief, in direct response to the Harley Seventy-Four. At the time, the two bitter rivals were becoming obsessed with the idea of wresting market leadership from one another, a battle that endured for nearly 20 years.

Singles & Fours

Despite its earlier experiences with small bikes, Indian seemed determined to sell one, and in 1926 came up with the Franklin-designed Prince, a 350cc (21cu in) sidevalve single that owed much to British practice. Small, light, economical and easy to ride, the Prince had much to recommend it and sold fairly well in America, though the hoped-for exports to Britain were to be dashed by new tariff barriers. Franklin also designed an ohv version for racing (Indian was at last winning races again despite the Harley-Davidson onslaught), and even a few overhead-cam prototypes were built. In

A 1924 Indian Chief. Sidevalve V-twins were to see Indian through to the end

A 1924 Indian Chief. It was a nice bike, but Harley-Davidson was fast catching up

The 1938 1265cc (77cu in) Indian 438. Note the beautiful detailing (right)

1927, Indian bought the remains of the Ace Motorcycle Company, which had built the four-cylinder Henderson. Meanwhile, the Scout was enlarged to 750cc (45.8cu in) in response to Excelsior's very fast Super X. The Scout 45, or 101, was the result, and backed up the Excelsior in forming a new class with almost the same performance as the big twins, but in a smaller, lighter package. It had great success in oval track racing and, like its predecessor, sold well. The four-cylinder Ace had been revived as

well, and by 1929 had a new in-house chassis as the Indian Four. In fact, there were several changes to the original Ace; capacity increased, there was a five-bearing crankshaft and new cylinder head. It gave Indian a big range of bikes, from the 350cc Prince to 1265cc Four, while the 101 Scout was the best-selling bike on the market.

Despite all of this, the American motorcycle market as a whole continued to decline, which encouraged Indian's owners

to spend what little profits there were on attempts at diversification by using an increasingly underused factory for other projects. Outboard motors, aeroplanes, a small car – all came to nothing and left the company very short of capital. It was hardly surprising then, that in the aftermath of the Wall Street Crash, Indian changed hands three times in the space of a year. A saviour arrived in the form of wealthy industrialist E. Paul duPont, who assumed a majority shareholding with the

idea of using Springfield to produce aero-engines. With the Depression continuing to bite, the plan came to nothing but duPont, unlike the fly-by-night investors, hung on and succeeded in turning Indian round. Hard times were to come before this was achieved, and in 1933 Indian built a mere 1,667 bikes.

Costs were cut by standardizing the same basic frame for Scout, Chief and Four, while the Prince frame was used for the 500cc (30.5cu in) Scout Pony and

ABOVE: Ed Kretz on his Indian racer

BELOW: Another Ed Kretz race bike

Depression, with just a hiccup in 1936 when the engine was changed to a side inlet/overhead exhaust-valve layout. It may or may not have worked better, but ruined the looks of the motor. By popular demand, it reverted to ioe after a couple of years, and then survived up to 1941, increasingly out on a limb and serving a tiny sector of the market. There was still a small following for this smooth, quiet, civilized motorcycle, but not enough to resume production of it after the war. In the late 1930s, the recovery continued, but although Indian finally matched Harley's output in 1939, it would never again reach the production heights of its early days. Nor was there any sign of an ohv twin to meet Harley-Davidson's successful Knucklehead. Perhaps, by this time, Indian had finally settled for second place.

Still, the war provided fresh impetus, particularly when France ordered 5,000 Chief sidecar outfits. However, the final batch of 2,000 never made it, though whether they ended up at the bottom of the Atlantic or not was never finally confirmed. But the factory was too rundown after years of underuse to capture the lion's share of military contracts. There was a militarized Chief and the M1, a lightweight 221cc (13cu in) sidevalve designed to be dropped into battle zones by parachute. The 841 was different again: impressed by Rommel's BMWs in North Africa, the army was insisting on shaft-drive, and Indian's transverse 90-degree V-twin was the result. It was a sidevalve 750, with four-speed gearbox and that shaft-drive, and over 10,000 were built. Less exotic was the 640B, basically a detuned Sport Scout in military guise.

750cc Motoplane. But one of duPont's finest legacies came in the form of paint. Part of his industrial empire encompassed the manufacture of paint, and consequently Indians became available in an unheard-of range of 24 different colours where the previous choice had been the traditional Indian red, or nothing. It transformed the appeal of the bikes, and Harley-Davidson had no choice but to follow suit. There was also a move towards streamlined art deco-like styling, with deep, graceful mudguards and rounded flowing tanks (the former not until 1940).

Motorcycling was discovering a new elegance, but there were mechanical changes too; the Sport Scout was the latest in the middleweight line and in 1935, along with the Chief, received the Y engine, which signified aluminium cylinder heads and barrels. And there was a three-wheeled Dispatch Tow, to compete with Harley-Davidson's similar Servi-car.

The Four kept going right through the

1946, and Indian returns to its pre-war V-twins

A 1943 militarized Indian. The transverse 841 V-twin was very different, and was designed from scratch

LEFT: A 1949 Indian Chief

ABOVE: A 1969 Indian Velo 500

Last Gasps ... then Revival?

Shortly after the war ended, E. Paul duPont sold Indian to the industrialist Ralph Rogers. Although duPont had apparently lost interest by this time, the company owed as much to him as it did to Hendee and Hedström, for he had kept it going right through the Depression when many would have given up. Ralph Rogers had great hopes for Indian, believing he could revive it with a combination of the traditional Chief and new European-style lightweights. In the short term, the 1941 Chief went back into production, with the addition of the 841's girder fork. For the future, Ralph Rogers bought the Torque Manufacturing Company which had single- and vertical-twin lightweights under development and

the whole enterprise was moved to Springfield. Rogers was a shrewd man and after researching the market predicted that smaller, lighter singles and twins would be the next growth area in the United States.

Sadly, when the long-awaited 220cc (13cu in) Arrow and 440cc (27cu in) Scout finally appeared in mid-1948, they simply weren't a match for the BSAs, Triumphs and Nortons. They actually looked spot-on, with telescopic forks, hand clutch and foot gearchange, just like the imports. But they lost out in engine capacity against the 250/500 opposition, were rushed into final production, and were poorly made to boot. Oil leaks, difficulty in starting and ignition problems ensued. The real tragedy was that the small bikes had absorbed a huge

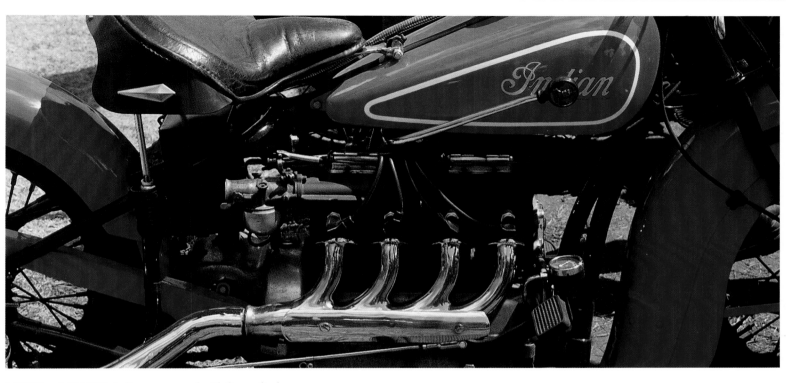

ABOVE and BELOW: Indian persevered with four cylinders

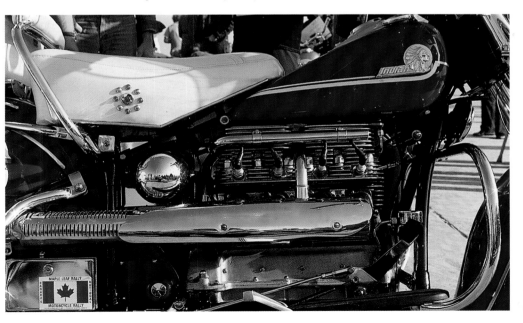

motor and telescopic forks. Meanwhile, the British-built Brockhouse Brave, a sidevalve 250, was imported to replace the home-built singles. None of this was enough, however, and the Warrior was dropped in 1952, while the Big Chief finally rolled over and died the following year. Harley-Davidson had finally won the contest.

However, this wasn't the end of the Indian name, even though some uses for it in the next 20 years would cause palpitations in the hearts of diehard enthusiasts. After the Brockhouse Brave fell by the wayside, there was an arrangement with Royal Enfield to badge its 250/350/500cc singles as Indians for the American market, which lasted until 1959. The model names were suitably Americanized as well, so the Meteor 700 became the Trailblazer or Apache, the 250 single Hounds Arrow, and so on. There was even an Enfield badged as the Indian Chief – sacrilege!

Then the name lapsed for a few years before an ex-Indian dealer revived it in 1967 with a mini-scooter, the Papoose, which was imported first from Britain, then from Italy. This was followed by the 50cc (3cu in) Bambino (a size similar to the Honda Monkey Bike) and in the early seventies by the off-road Junior Cross, which used a Jawa/CZ 50cc engine, and 100, 125 and 175 versions followed. Floyd Clymer (a publisher and ex-racing driver, who had undertaken to breathe new life into the company) was nothing if not eclectic, and his 1969 Indian Velo 500 used a combination of Italian cycle parts with some of the last Velocette 500cc singles. Sadly, Clymer died in 1970, but the Indian baton passed to a Los Angeles lawyer named Alan Newman. His venture was truly international, with Indian minibikes using

amount of money ($6.5 million was mentioned) which could have been spent updating the Chief. The faithful V-twin was still selling in reasonable numbers (having been Indian's sole product until the tiddlers came along) and prototypes had been built with telescopic forks and foot change; now, however, there were just not sufficient funds to put them into production. In the face of all this, Ralph Rogers was forced to resign, and manufacture passed to the Titeflex Corporation (part of the Atlas group which had helped finance Rogers' venture). There were some useful improvements in that the Scout twin gained power and reliability as the 500cc (30.5cu in) Warrior, while the Chief returned with an enlarged 1340cc (82cu in)

OPPOSITE: The 1953 Chief was the last of the 'true' Indians

ABOVE: The Indian Woodsman, a rebadged Royal Enfield

Italian engines in a Taiwanese chassis. After three years, however, he had had enough and sold the name to a bank, which in turn allowed its use by the American Moped Company, its project being a Taiwanese four-stroke moped, the Indian 'Four'. All was quiet for a while until the mid-1980s when American entrepreneurs claimed rights to the name, both having plans for a new modern Chief. Neither succeeded. Then in 1994 the name was bought by Australian businessman Marits Hayim-Langridge. He commissioned the late John Britten (builder of a successful V-twin race bike) to develop a new range of V-twins to be produced in America in 1998. Like all recent plans, this came to nothing, but the good news was that in February 1999 the name had been bought by a Canadian firm for $17 million. The latest owners promise a new Indian Chief for later in the year, first with an S&S V-twin, and with the company's own engine the following year. Could this mean the long awaited rebirth of Indian? If recent experience is any guide, don't hold your breath!

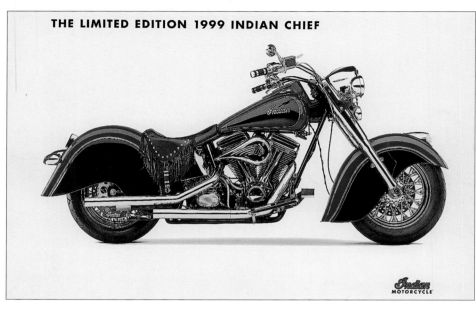

THE LIMITED EDITION 1999 INDIAN CHIEF

Sales brochure for the 1999 Indian Chief – reborn at last?

Or should we stick to the memories?

INDUS *Germany 1924–27*
Had front and rear leaf-sprung suspension, with bought-in single-cylinder engines from Kühne, Küchen and JAP.

INTRAMOTOR *Italy 1971–81*
Produced Minarelli-engined mopeds and a selection of 122cc (7cu in) off-road machines.

INVICTA *England 1902–06*
An assembler who utilized Minerva and Kelecom engines.

INVICTA *England 1913–23*
Used 269cc (16cu in) Villiers, 499cc (30cu inch) sv Abingdon and 346/678cc (21/41cu inch) sv JAP engines, the bikes having been built in the Francis-Barnett factory.

INVICTA *Italy 1951–54*
74–123cc (4.5–7.5cu in) two-strokes.

IRESA *Spain 1956–59*
Used Spanish licence-built Villiers units up to 198cc (12cu in).

IRIS *England 1902–06*
A 5hp water-cooled V-twin, with hand starter and friction clutch, which is unusual.

IRIS *Italy 1952–53*
Utilized 123cc (7.5cu in) Ilo two-stroke power.

IRUNA *Spain 1953–59*
Built scooters with in-house 123cc (7.5cu in) two-strokes.

ISLO *Mexico 1958–*
Began with a 175cc (11cu in) scooter-style bike assembled from Italian parts. Later used 48–248cc (3–15cu in) two-strokes, built under licence from Sachs. Also sold in the U.S.A. under the Cooper badge.

ISOMOTO *Italy 1949–64*
Used its own double-pistoned two-stroke engines of up to 248cc (15cu in), plus 123cc and 173cc (7.5 and 11cu in) ohv engines.

ITALA *Italy 1933–39*
Was an importer of French Train engines, so used the Train 98cc (6cu in) two-stroke first, then progressed to bigger Chaise and Python engines.

ITALEMMEZETA *Italy 1958–66*
Used MZ engines of 98–248cc (6–15cu in) in Italian cycle parts.

ITALJET *Italy 1966–*
Established by Leopoldo Tartarini, who used CZ, Velocette and Triumph engines in his own frames, as well as Minarelli, MZ and Yamaha units later on. Also built Floyd Clymer's Indian Velocette in 1970 and concentrated on sub-125cc trials and

motocross bikes after that, including children's off-road machines. There was also a road-going two-stroke twin, the 124cc (8cu in) Buccaneer. By the mid-1990s, and still owned by the Tartarini family, Italjet was now making scooters and doing very well out of a growing market, planning to double production to 40,000 bikes in 1996 to make it second only to Piaggio in Italian scooter production. The company has sought to differentiate its scooters from the competition with the sports-style hub-centre-steered Formula 50 and 125, the retro-style Velocifero and radical Dragster.

ITAR *Czechoslovakia 1921–29*
Its mainstay was a 746cc (45.5cu in) sv flat twin, built for the Czechoslovak army as well as for civilians. A 346cc (21cu in) single failed to reach production, but JAP-engined singles did.

BELOW: 1999 Italjet Dragster D50LC Race Replica

BELOW: 1999 Italjet Torpedo 125

ABOVE and ABOVE RIGHT: A 150, with its twin-pistoned two-stroke

ITOM *Italy 1945–68*
Started with a 48cc (3cu in) clip-on and progressed to mopeds and 65cc (4cu in) sports lightweights.

IVEL *England 1901–05*
Utilized De Dion and MMC engines.

IVER-JOHNSON *U.S.A. 1907–15*
Produced singles and V-twins up to 1090cc (66.5cu in).

IVO LOLA RIBAR *Yugoslavia 1956*
Made Vespa scooters under licence.

IVY *England 1908–32*
First used Precision and JAP engines, then its own two-strokes. Later resumed production, once again with two-stroke and JAP options.

IXION *England 1901–03*
Used De Dion and MMC engines.

IXION *England 1910–23*
Used various bought-in engines from Abingdon, Precision and Peco.

IZH *Former U.S.S.R. 1933–*
One of the oldest Soviet motorcycle factories is at Izhevsk, and is home to a number of marques. Earliest bikes were 746 and 1200cc (45.5 and 73cu in) V-twins, followed by 198cc (12cu in) two-strokes and 498cc (30cu in) ohc singles. From 1938 there was the DKW-based 348cc two-stroke single (the Ish), with 18bhp. It was reintroduced in 1946 as the Planeta, and in 1961 was joined by a 350cc (21cu in) twin, the Jupiter, with 25bhp at 4,600rpm.

J

JAC *Czechoslovakia 1929–32*
An interesting 498cc (30cu in) single-cylinder sleeve-valved unit-designed machine with shaft-drive and a welded frame of pressed steel. Designed by J. A. Cvach, the machines had a leaf-sprung fork, a low saddle position and a triangular fuel tank between saddle and gearbox.

JACK SPORT *France 1927–31*
349/498cc (21/30cu in) four-strokes.

JAK *Germany 1922–25*
Used 119–173cc (7–11cu in) bought-in two-strokes from DKW and Bekamo.

JALE *Germany 1923–25*
Air- and water-cooled 170cc (10cu in) two-strokes.

JAMATHI *The Netherlands 1969–71*
Sporting 49cc (3cu in) two-strokes.

JAMES *England 1902–66*
Harry James set up on his own quite late in life when already well-established as works manager of a Birmingham engineering works, at an age when most contemporaries would be looking forward to a comfortable retirement. His James Cycle Company was successful, and in 1902 he did what so many cycle manufacturers were doing and tentatively ventured into the motorization market.

The James version was entirely conventional, with a bought-in Minerva engine clipped to the front downtube, and was belt-driven. But 1908 saw something very avant-garde indeed. A man named P.L. Renouf designed for James a motorcycle

OPPOSITE and ABOVE: A 1928 James 350SS

ABOVE: Early James machines seemed modern by the standards of their times

BELOW: A 1949 James utility – leisurely transport with a sidecar

that thoroughly bristled with innovation. Both wheels were carried on stub axles, and there was hub-centre-steering: the 600cc (37cu in) single had concentric inlet and exhaust valves, and internally expanding brakes, probably the first bike to be so fitted. With the exception of the brakes, few of these features lasted long but one became a James trademark, i.e. the cylinder cooling fins were staggered in a 'pineapple' arrangement.

James followed this in 1911 with an up-to-the-minute all-chain transmission with two-speed gearbox and multi-plate clutch, followed by a whole array of models in the next few years. There was a small two-stroke in 1913, a 500cc (30.5cu in) sidevalve V-twin in 1914, a little autocycle after the war, and eventually an ohv version of the 500 twin. Perhaps it was the expense

of building this wide range of engines that persuaded James to stop and do what many small British manufacturers did – buy in from Villiers. In fact, the decision dictated the subsequent James policy of building up to 250cc (15cu in) only, and the firm's motorized bicycle of 1938 was a result of Villiers' launch of a 98cc (6cu in) autocycle engine of which 6,000 were made for essential private transport during World War II. The company also sold a little 125 to the army, the ML (Military Lightweight).

In fact, when civilian production resumed in 1946, it was merely with these two models – the fuel-sipping Autocycle (ideal for petrol-rationed Britain) and a civilianized version of the ML in maroon and grey. As Villiers' post-war engine range expanded, so did James' motorcycles, though in 1951 the company was taken over

A 1935 Jawa 350cc (21cu in)

by Associated Motor Cycles. As part of the group, James was obliged to use the corporate two-stroke engine in its Cadet, Cavalier and Commodore, all of which used partly pressed steel frames. There was also a belated attempt to capture a slice of the growing scooter market, but although the 150cc (9cu in) James offering had its good points (notably a low centre of gravity and generous luggage space) it had much in common with other British scooters in being too heavy, too clumsy and too late.

Still, until the advent of Bultaco, there was competition success for the trials Commando and scrambler Cotswold, and the road range was topped by the good-looking Sports Captain and 250cc Superswift twin. However, this was no match for the new Japanese lightweights streaming onto the market. Even if James hadn't been sucked under by the AMC collapse of 1966, it is unlikely that it could have survived on its own.

JAP *England 1904–08*
One of the most prolific engine manufacturers of all, with capacities ranging from 123–1098cc (7.5–67cu in). The demand was such that JAP stopped building complete bikes in 1908, but the engine factory was taken over by Villiers after World War II.

ABOVE and ABOVE RIGHT: 1929 Jawa 500cc (30.5cu in)

BELOW: This makeshift three-wheeler (photographed in Romania by Roger Fogg) is a CZ, produced when it later merged with Jawa

JAVON *Germany 1929–32*
Used 198cc and 498cc (12 and 30cu in)
JAP singles.

JAWA *Czechoslovakia 1929–*
The name Jawa derives from JAnacek-
WAnderer. Arms industrialist F. Janacek
wished to get into the motorcycle market
and bought the rights to the German
Wanderer, a 498cc (30cu in) ohv single with
shaft-drive and pressed steel frame. It was
underdeveloped, and various teething
troubles prevented its commercial success.
However, the fledgling Jawa concern was
saved by the arrival of English designer
George Patchett, who set about creating a
successful racer, and by the introduction of
a 173cc (11cu in) Villiers-powered machine
in 1932. Patchett also designed 346cc
(21cu in) sv and ohv road bikes for Jawa,

ABOVE: A CZ 175 Sports　　　　*BELOW: A later CZ 175 trail bike*

250/350 two-stroke twins were Jawa's main product from the 1960s on

Czech designer Jozif produced a 98cc (6cu in) two-stroke. After the war, Jawa was nationalized and 250 two-stroke singles and 350 twins were introduced which have formed the backbone of Jawa's output since. There were still sophisticated dohc racers (some supercharged), and an ohc 500cc (30.5cu in) twin in the mid-1950s. Jawa enjoyed much success in six-day trials, motocross and speedway after the war, but its mainstay bikes were the 250/350 two-strokes, plus a 49cc (3cu in) moped.

JB-LOUVET *France 1926–30*
Made Aubier-Dunne-powered 173/246cc (11/15cu in) two-strokes and 348/498cc (21/30cu in) JAP engines were also used.

JD *England 1920–26*
Made by Bowden, the JD was a 116cc (7cu in) clip-on. It was also supplied with a strengthened bicycle frame.

JEAN THOMANN *France 1920–30*
98–248cc (6–15cu in) two-strokes and a 499cc (30cu in) ohv single with external flywheel.

JE-BE *Germany late 1950s–late-1960s*
98/123cc (6/7.5cu in) Sachs-powered two-strokes for the U.S. market, the name inspired by its importer, Joe Berliner.

JEECY-VEA *Belgium 1923–27*
Specialized in flat twins of up to 746cc (45.5cu in), all bought-ins. King Albert of the Belgians rode one.

JEFFERSON *U.S.A. 1911–14*
Front and rear suspension appeared on this development of the PEM.

BELOW and RIGHT: A rare 1955 500cc (30.5cu in) Jawa overhead-camshaft twin

JEHU *England 1901–c.1910*
Used Minerva and MMC engines as well as its own 2.25–3hp units.

JELINEK *Czechoslovakia 1904–07*
Utilized Minerva, Orion or Fafnir power.

JES *England 1910–24*
Before 1914, there was early use of ohv engines, then came two-strokes and bigger Blackburne singles before takeover by Connaught.

JESMOND *England 1899–1907*
A choice of De Dion, MMC and Sarolea power was on offer.

JFK *Czechoslovakia 1923–26*
An advanced ohc 348cc (21cu in) single, designed by J.F. Koch.

JH *England 1913–15*
Utilized JAP, Villiers and MAG engines.

JHC *Germany 1922–24*
Used own 183cc (11cu in) three-port two-stroke.

JNU *England 1920–22*
Utilized a 312cc (19cu in) two-stroke Dalm engine but production of the motorcycles was limited.

JNZ *New Zealand 1960–63*
Jawas and CZs assembled in New Zealand; also known as N-ZETA.

JOERNS *U.S.A. 1910–15*
The 996cc (61cu in) Cyclone was probably the first ohc V-twin built in reasonable numbers.

JONGHI *France 1931–56*
Produced 348cc (21cu in) sv singles first, then ohc singles of 173–348cc (11–21cu in).

JOOS *Germany 1900–07*
Built flat-twin motors at first, later complete bikes powered by Fafnir singles and V-twins.

JOUCLARD *France 1903–07*
1.5/2.25hp singles.

JOYBIKE *England 1959–60*
Scooter-like lightweight with 49cc (3cu in) Trojan or 70cc (4cu in) JAP engines.

JSL *Germany 1923–25*
Choice of own 132/180cc (8/11cu in) two-strokes or DKW's 206cc (12.6cu in) unit.

JUCKES *England 1910–26*
Built all its own gearboxes and engines, from 269–399cc (16–24cu in) two-strokes and a 348cc (21cu in) ohv single.

JUERGENSEN *Denmark 1904–14*
Built Humber machines under licence.

JUÉRY *France 1931–39*
Built its own engines, but also offered Chaise 346/498cc (21/30cu in) sv and ohv units.

JUHÖ *Germany 1922–24*
Produced in-house 148cc (9cu in) sv or 195cc (12cu in) two-strokes.

JULES *Czechoslovakia 1929–34*
A 120cc (7cu in) two-stroke clip-on was made, together with Praga bicycles.

JUNAK *Poland 1956–64*
In-house 247/347cc (15/21cu in) four-stroke singles.

JUNCKER *The Netherlands 1932–35*
Used 98–198cc (6–12cu in) Ilo or Villiers engines.

JUNCKER *France 1935–37*
Stainless and Aubier-Dunne-powered two-strokes of 98–147cc (6–9cu in).

JUNIOR *Italy 1924–35*
Began with own two-strokes of up to 346cc (21cu in), later buying in JAP and Blackburne four-strokes.

JUNO *England 1911–23*
Engines were from Villiers, Precision and JAP (770cc/47cu inch V-twin), with frames from Sun.

JUPP *England 1921–24*
A step-through frame, rear suspension and 269cc (16cu in) Liberty two-stroke made this a cross between a scooter and a motorcycle.

K

KADI *Germany 1924–30*
Used own 198cc (12cu in) sv and the Küchen three-valve ohc 498cc (30cu in) single.

KAHENA *Mexico 1992–*
VW Beetle-engined, like the Amazonas, but a more modern, compact design with single-sided swinging arm and twin-spar frame.

KANTO *Japan 1957–60*
Just one model, a 124cc (8cu in) two-stroke.

KAPTEIN *The Netherlands 1938–51*
Fitted four-stroke engines and other parts from Motobécane.

KARÜ *Germany 1922–24*
A 398cc (24cu in) Bosch-Douglas flat twin.

KATAKURA *Japan 1958–c.1962*
120–200cc (7–12cu in) two-stroke singles and twins.

KATHO *Germany 1923–25*
Used 198cc (12cu in) sv Alba engines.

KAUBA *Austria 1953–55*
Sachs-engined scooters to 124cc (8cu in).

KAWASAKI *Japan 1960–*
This, the fourth of the Japanese Big Four manufacturers, came late to motorcycles and didn't built its first complete bike until 1960, even though it could trace its roots back to the 19th century. But although, in Europe at least, Kawasaki has sometimes been overshadowed and outsold by its three well known competitors, the motorcycles bearing this badge are the product of a giant Japanese corporation – a classic *zaibatsu* – that makes everything from helicopters to gas turbines to recycling machines. Even the English Channel Tunnel boring machine was built by the 'Big K', not to mention the famous Japanese Shinkensen Bullet train.

Shozo Kawasaki founded a shipyard at Tsukiji, Tokyo in 1878, and another at Hyogo just three years later. He was an

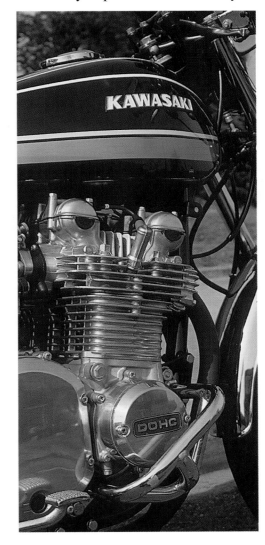

The Kawasaki 900 ZI was designed to outshine Honda's CB750, and it did

early player in Japan's rapid transition towards modernization which was beginning to gather pace around this time. Kawasaki Dockyard both contributed to and benefited from this process, able to diversify into railway equipment in 1906, then into steam turbines, then (just 15 years after the Wright brothers' first flight)

aircraft. Already, the foundations were being laid for Kawasaki's enduring success, which was diversification into all branches of engineering.

Perhaps it was this versatility that allowed Kawasaki to recover so quickly after 1945. Never a one-product company, it was able to benefit from the general

striving for reconstruction as a Japan, devastated by war, sought to rebuild itself. As Soichiro Honda was to discover, one of the first demands of early post-war Japan, once the basics of life had been met, was for some form of motorized transport. The country was still a generation away from mass car use, but powered two-wheelers

(as long as they were cheap and reliable) were just the thing.

Kawasaki refrained from plunging straight into this market, but began by supplying engines to other manufacturers, the first being a 148cc (9cu in) ohv four-stroke, complete with four-speed gearbox. It was such a success that different capacities soon followed, and within a few years a new Kawasaki subsidiary was busy building engines for a large range of customers. Among them was Meguro, which was selling (among other things) a licence-built version of the BSA A7/A10. Meguro proved to be the Big K's route into motorcycle manufacture, being absorbed by the giant in 1960/61. At the same time, an all-new assembly plant was being built in Akashi, dedicated to building bikes, and in 1962 produced its first product with a Kawasaki badge, the B8. There was nothing unusual about the it. It was a straightforward, sensible 125cc (8cu in) two-stroke and was, like almost every other Japanese motorcycle made at the time, a utility product. However, an early attempt to export the B8 to the U.S. met with disappointing sales. What the Americans wanted was something to rival the British bikes and Harley-Davidson – something large.

Up a Blind Alley – then Success

Unlikely as it may seem, Kawasaki had (or thought it had) something suitable right away. It had inherited Meguro's BSA-based parallel twin, which offered a quick route into the big bike market. No matter that even BSA had recently dropped the pre-unit twin as outdated (it had first seen the light of day in 1946), Kawasaki launched a 624cc (38cu in) version named the W1 in 1966. With 50bhp at 6,500rpm it was at least able to compete with younger British twins, and it looked and rode much like a pre-unit BSA. Kawasaki persevered with the W1, and it actually survived for five years in one guise or another, notably in the W1SS and street

ABOVE: A KH-series bike, the later two-stroke triple

BELOW: KM90, a 90cc (5.5cu in) single-cylinder two-stroke midibike with a 5-speed gear box

scrambler-style W2TT Commander.

However, with the best will in the world, the Meguro/BSA was never going to form the basis of Kawasaki's success. That came from something launched the same year as the W1. It was a small, highly tuned two-stroke that set new standards for small bike performance – the A1 Samurai. The A1 couldn't have been more different from the W1, but it was to be the first of a long line of high-performance two-strokes that would put Kawasaki firmly on the motorcycle map. It was unusual in that the 247cc (15cu in) twin used a disc-valve, which of necessity meant a side-mounted carburettor; but Kawasaki avoided excessive width by mounting the alternator behind the crankshaft rather than on one end. Together with a 338cc (21cu in) version (the Avenger) the Samurai sold well in the U.S., and Kawasaki learnt an important lesson regarding the 1960s motorcycle market – that performance sold.

Kawasaki responded in no uncertain terms with the three-cylinder H1, the Mach III. The year of the Mach III's launch, 1968, was particularly memorable for the birth of what soon became known as the superbike; but it also saw three very different interpretations of that concept. From BSA/Triumph came the three-cylinder, four-stroke Rocket Three/Trident, while Honda's CB750 added a new level of sophistication with more power than the British bike, and disc brake, electric start and overhead cam as well. But Kawasaki's offering was different again. Despite being a 'mere' 500cc (30.5cu in), it equalled the 740cc (45cu in) Triumph in power and was lighter. Not surprisingly, it had stunning

ABOVE: The Estrella 250 (1991) was a real retro bike

acceleration, though it also gained a reputation for less than stable handling: not for the first time in motorcycling, the Mach III was a bike with an engine ahead of its chassis!

Perhaps the Mach III was a bit too fierce for its own good, and it certainly mellowed a little over the years, being gradually detuned from its original 60bhp to 52bhp by 1976. What it did do, of course, was to bring Kawasaki to everyone's attention, and it was successful enough to spawn a whole family of two-stroke triples: the S1 250cc (15cu in), S2 350cc (21cu in) and 399cc (24cu in) S3. Plus, of course, the amazing H2 or Mach IV, an enlarged Mach III powered by a 748cc (46cu in) version of the triple, which produced 74bhp at 6,800rpm and had an alleged top speed of 209km/h (130mph). It

was a fitting climax to the two-stroke era of raw performance and horrendous fuel consumption. But even as the Mach IV went on sale, Kawasaki was already close to launching its real flagship for the next decade, the Z1.

A New Era

Exciting though its manic two-strokes were, Kawasaki had no intention of abandoning four-stroke engines. By the late 1960s, the W1 650 was sadly outdated, and work began on a successor. It couldn't have been more different for the company had decided that its new flagship would not merely be a competitive bike but one that would be bigger and faster than anything comparable. So when the Honda CB750 appeared in late 1968, the prototype Kawasaki was rapidly upgraded to 900cc

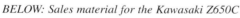

BELOW: Sales material for the Kawasaki Z650C

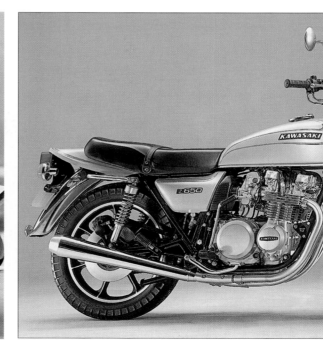

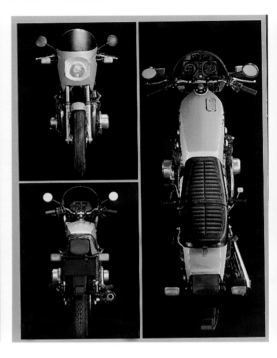

ABOVE: Sales material for the original Z1-R

BELOW: The 1999 Drifter (800 or 1500cc) aped the Indian look

(55cu in). The Honda had a single overhead camshaft, so the secret Kawasaki had two. The Honda produced 67bhp, the Z1 had 82.

Here was something with the performance of the fearsome Mach IV, but which was also easy to ride, happy at low speeds and relatively simple to service. Intensive testing of prototypes (mainly in America, which was after all the biggest market for this type of bike) ensured it was free of teething troubles as well. In fact, the Z1's air-cooled 903cc dohc engine became something of a design classic, forming the basis, not only of a long line of big road bikes, but also of much success in endurance and drag racing as well.

While all this was going on, Kawasaki had not forgotten its roots in smaller, utility bikes. The original B8 had hung on until 1966, but the year before that came the

ABOVE: A KH100 EX commuter

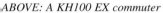
BELOW: KZ1000 ST

ABOVE: The Z750 four was overshadowed by the big Z1000s

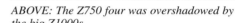

85cc (5cu in) J1, first of a long line of disc-valved two-stroke singles. It was soon replaced with a 90cc version, which in turn led to the long-running KC90 and KC100 commuter bikes. At complete odds with the glamorous, high performance bikes at the top of the range, these simple two-strokes were reliable and well-priced and, of course, able to bask in the reflected glory of their less utilitarian brothers. A little more exciting were the two-stroke trail bikes which Kawasaki, like its competitors, designed in response to (or perhaps as encouragement to) the new American craze for off-roading, for leisure as much as for sport. This market demanded something very different from the big, heavy four-stroke 'street scramblers' of the time, which even if they did venture off-road were too much of a handful for all but the brave.

Instead, the new lightweights allowed novice off-roaders to have a bit of fun on the dirt without fear of over-stretching themselves. Kawasaki's contribution came in 1969, with two 100cc (6cu in) trail bikes, two 250s, and a 346cc (21cu in) single known as 'Bighorn'. With 33bhp, the Bighorn was one of the most powerful 'trailies' you could buy, and was on sale until the mid-1970s.

A plethora of trail bikes followed as the market continued to grow, notably the 175 Bushwhacker and 250 Bison (which later became the less flamboyantly named KE175 and KE250 respectively). These were all two-strokes, of course, but in 1978 Kawasaki departed from tradition and unveiled two small four-stroke singles. The KL250 was the trail bike and was to survive until replaced by the dohc KLR in 1984.

A GPZ1100 of the 1980s

ABOVE: An early 650 twin on the production line

BELOW: Z1-R – a late seventies classic

Meanwhile, the Z200 was a mildly-tuned four-stroke single that was quite a luxury commuter, with electric start and a balancer shaft to reduce vibration. Still, the two-stroke AR50, 80 and 125 of a few years later underlined Kawasaki's commitment to the two-stroke engine. They had sharp styling and were well specified, with Kawasaki's own Uni-Trak (monoshock) rear suspension system, a front disc brake and 21bhp from the full-powered liquid-cooled 125. A KMX125 was the trail bike version, which arrived in 1986.

Four-Stroke Expansion

The Z1, then the Z900, had been great successes; but they left a big gap in Kawasaki's range with the advent of the KH500, which was serving an increasingly specialist market (the days of the big two-stroke would soon be over). The logical thing to do was to follow the competition and come up with medium-sized four-stroke fours to capitalize on the Z bike's

success, which is exactly what Kawasaki did

First along was the 652cc (40cu in) Z650 in 1976, which was notable for virtually resurrecting a near-forgotten capacity class (650s were part of the folk-memory of old British twins), but now there was a torquey, easy to ride all-rounder, without the weight and intimidation of the bigger four-cylinder bikes, but still with reasonable performance. The 500 class had never gone away, and Kawasaki duly came up with a Z500 in 1979, plus a smaller Z400 version as well. Logically, a four-cylinder Z750 followed on in 1980, with 79bhp at 9,500rpm. It wasn't actually the first 750-4 sold by Kawasaki – that honour went to a Japanese market version of the original Z1.

In fact, Kawasaki seemed to be approaching the mainstream, producing bikes ever closer to those of the other three Japanese manufacturers. There was good reason for this, with the two-stroke triples losing favour, but the company still decided to hedge its bets and carry on offering the KH250/400/500 (as they now were)

ABOVE and RIGHT: A sales brochure for the Kawasaki 1987 range of motorcycles

alongside the new-for-1974 Z400. Perhaps it was being in parallel with the more sporting KH series that dictated the Z400's role as a sound all-rounder. Its sohc 398cc (24cu in) twin produced sufficient power for a near-100mph top speed, but hardly added up to exciting motorcycling. Still, it was reliable and reasonably economical, with all the usual mod cons now expected of a budget bike, with electric start, disc brake and twin helmet locks. It also had balancer shafts to help quell the parallel twin's vibration. Its only major change came in 1980 when it was bored out to 443cc (27cu in). More interesting, from an historical point of view, was the 745cc (45cu in) Z750 twin of 1977; interesting, because no other Japanese rival was building a 750 twin for the road. Yamaha's XS650 had sold quite well as a more modern equivalent of the traditional British twin, and logically a 750 should have done so too. However, the public now seemed to prefer four cylinders for an engine this large, and the Z750 was not a success.

At the other end of the scale, Kawasaki's smallest road-going four-stroke twin certainly was. The Z250 Scorpion faced very similar competition from Honda,

BELOW: The Z1300 with six cylinders and 1300cc (79cu in)

Yamaha and Suzuki, but was a full 10kg (22lb) lighter than Honda's Superdream, and with a claimed maximum of 60km/h (97mph) was faster. It did well in Britain where, at the time, learners could ride a 250cc bike with no power limit. The Z250 later grew into the oddly-sized GPZ305, which was also distinguishable from the ordinary by virtue of its toothed belt-drive. Two steps up from the 305 was the GPZ500S, which first appeared in 1987. Following the lead of the new big Kawasakis, the new twin used a liquid-cooled engine with four valves per cylinder and twin overhead camshafts; the similarity was hardly surprising as the 500S was no more nor less than half of a GPZ1000 RX four-cylinder engine. With 60bhp at 9,800rpm and relatively light weight (169kg/373lb), it offered something approaching four-cylinder performance in a slimmer, handier package. It also boasted Uni-Trak rear suspension, which was patented by Kawasaki as one of the first 'monoshock' systems, and used a single spring/damper unit to control the swinging arm rather than the usual two. The top of the damper was attached to the frame, the bottom to the swinging arm via a compound linkage. First used on KR250 racers in 1976, it went on to appear on most of the Big K's bigger road bikes. Today, monoshock rear systems of one sort or another are almost universal.

Something else very common in today's market is the cruiser or custom bike, straight out of the factory. Harley-Davidson has been customizing for years, but Kawasaki was the first of the Japanese Big Four to wake up to this potentially lucrative market. The trend had been started by

The 1984 GPZ900R set new standards in its class

Kawasaki's U.S. importer, which took it on itself to sell a few Z900s with custom parts ready fitted. The factory soon responded with 'custom' versions of the Z750 (both four and twin), Z250C, 440 and Z1000. In each case, the formula was the same – higher bars, extra chrome, a stepped seat and different paintwork; but Kawasaki went on to produce factory customs which were models in their own right, notably the EN450 (the engine unique to that model)

and the Z900-powered ZL900 Eliminator. In the eighties, the trend began for customs (or cruisers, as they were increasingly called) to be designed from the ground up, with little in common with the sports road bikes. So came purpose-designed V-twins like the VN750 (later 800) and VN1500. The *raison d'être* for these bikes was to get as close as possible to the Harley style, albeit with added reliability and ease of riding. In that, they succeeded.

BELOW: The KLE500, a twin-cylinder trail bike

ABOVE: The nineties Cyclone looked to the past   *BELOW: The 1997 ER-5 was deservedly popular*

Racers

Remember Meguro? Kawasaki's early partner in the bike business had successfully competed in Japanese dirt-track racing in the 1950s, with a 500cc (30.5cu in) single. The effect wasn't lost on Kawasaki, which won the Japanese 125cc motocross championship as early as 1963. Track success took longer, and it wasn't until 1969 that it finally won a GP championship. Ironically, this was due to Englishman Dave Simmonds who had been taken on in 1967 to ride the 125cc (8cu in) two-stroke twin and, having sat out 1968 due to a serious accident, was loaned his old 125 for the 1969 season, together with a box of spares. Competing on a shoestring, he won eight of the GP rounds that year and clinched the championship.

It was the 500cc two-stroke triple that gave Kawasaki its first Production Racing successes in both the U.S. and Europe. The factory was even inspired to produce its own track version of the road bike, the H1-R, which managed 70bhp at 9,000rpm due to various tweaks here and there. Several successes followed until the 750cc triple took over as the H2-R, almost sweeping the board in America during the 1973 season. Better was to come as the new Z900 proved a natural for endurance racing. Frenchmen Georges Godier and Alain Genoud won the Endurance Championship in 1975, heralding a whole string of successes for big Kawasaki four-strokes in long-distance racing. Meanwhile, the 750 two-stroke had been liquid-cooled and was doing well in shorter races and Mick Grant won the Senior TT on one that year.

But Kawasaki still hadn't cracked the intermediate class until it came up with a

ABOVE: ZXR750 was an uncompromising race replica

BELOW: The ZZR series was a more civilized breed of sports tourers

tandem (cylinders fore-and-aft rather than side-by-side) two-stroke, which scored its first GP victory in the 1977 Dutch TT. The following year, Kork Ballington took both 250 and 350 GP titles on Kawasaki tandem twins. More 250/350 championships followed and a 500cc four (the KR500) for the top GP class. But the KR500 never achieved the same success, and Kawasaki pulled out of GP racing in 1982. In the 1990s, World Superbike racing has tended to overshadow the Grand Prix, and Kawasaki was an early competitor in this form of racing, which only achieved true world status in 1988. The four-cylinder ZXR750-R was a racing version of the road-going ZXR, and won various smaller Superbike championships before securing a WSB title in 1993. It was replaced by the ZX-7RR in 1996.

Of course, off-road competition had long been the source of success for Kawasaki, often under the Team Green label. There were motocross wins in the 250 and 400 classes in the early 1970s, and Jim Weinert won the American AMA championship in 1974. Although the company also competed in trials, it was motocross and enduro that remained the most successful arenas, with first air-cooled, then liquid-cooled, KDX 250s, 420s and others having sold well to private riders.

BELOW: The 1998 ZX9-R still sells well

The Big Fours

We left the biggest Kawasaki as a 900cc (55cu in) air-cooled four, but within a few years it was bored out to 1015cc (62cu in) to create the Z1000. The company seemed determined to offer its latest flagship in every conceivable form: the Z-1R was the café racer of the range, with the obligatory cockpit fairing. The Z1000H had no fairing

ABOVE: The ZXR750 gave way to the ZX7-R

but was the first production Kawasaki with fuel injection; it was electronically controlled, the precursor of the GPZ1100's digital fuel injection. Then there was the Z1000ST tourer, complete with shaft-drive, the price-leading Z1000J and the Z1000R, a road-going version of the bikes ridden by Eddie Lawson and others in the U.S. But the horsepower race continued, and Kawasaki responded on two fronts. The 750 Turbo was the standard Z750 four with the addition of a turbocharger (112bhp), while the 120bhp GPZ1100 used yet another enlargement of the air-cooled four, plus a Uni-Trak rear-end and anti-dive front forks. It was fast (over 209km/h/130mph) but, at 224kg (494lb), very heavy.

BELOW: The 1986 GPZ1000 RX

Just as the Z1 heralded a new era for Kawasaki in the early seventies, so did the GPZ900R ten years later. The big shift here was from air- to liquid-cooling. This might have been expected to add more weight to an already bulky bike, but in fact the new engine was physically smaller than the old one, as well as 5kg (11lb) lighter (though the GPZ900 actually weighed slightly more than the 1100). It produced 114bhp, only slightly less than the air-cooled 1100, though it was interesting that the company stuck with carburettors for its new sportster (fuel injection didn't yet offer sufficient advantages in the cost/benefit balance). No matter, the new GPZ could top 254km/h (158mph), whatever its fuel system, and was the first departure from the big one-

GPZ500S

DREAM MACHINE

A MAGIC CARPET RIDE

Lean, light, and packing a two-fisted punch of proven Kawasaki power, the all-new GPZ500S is ready to carry you wherever your imagination runs.

It's tractable and easy-to-handle. So whether you're letting the good times roll down city streets, highways, or twisting mountain roads, the GPZ's easy-going nature inspires new levels of confidence.

Then there's its high-tech engine. Sporty suspension systems. And aerodynamics slippery enough to deceive the wind.

So you get a performance package that's exciting for any rider to open up.

OUR SECRET FORMULA

We knew that to develop a 500cc powerplant with the kind of performance that Kawasaki is famous for, we would need to look beyond conventional means.

Inspiration came

from the GPZ1000RX—the world's fastest production motorcycle.

By cutting the big Four in half, we got exactly what we wanted—a high-flying Twin with all the right stuff:

Efficient liquid cooling. Eight quick-breathing valves. High-revving dual overhead cams. Exclusive semi-flat-slide carbs.

Technology that translates into proven reliability, a strong dose of easy-riding torque, and lots of high-performance fun.

THE ROAD IS YOURS

Weighing in at just 169kg the GPZ500S is lean enough to make every pony count.

Sophisticated Uni-Trak rear suspension keeps the wide tyre

tracking smoothly over the pavement, while a box-section high-tensile steel frame provides the strength for spirited cornering and braking.

The front disc brake is the best in the business. Featuring Kawasaki's exclusive Balanced Actuation Caliper (BAC), this new system delivers stronger stops with more precise feel.

And the super-nimble 16-inch wheels help you maneuver through the esses with the greatest of ease.

In short, the new GPZ500S offers you everything you'd expect in a high-tech sport bike.

And that's a dream come true.

- New radiator maximises liquid-cooled reliability.
- Cast alloy three-spoke wheels cut unsprung weight to help ensure cat-quick agility.
- Optional undercowling enhances the sleek sports styling.

All-new fairing-mounted instrument console is compact and easy-to-read.

With a smaller leading piston, the exclusive BAC caliper outperforms conventional dual-piston setups.

Uni-Trak rear suspension adjusts for optimum performance.

ABOVE and RIGHT: Sales material for the GPZ500S

BELOW: The GPX750R

litre plus sportsbikes to something more wieldy. When the last GPZ900Rs were sold in the mid-1990s, the world of hypersports motorcycles had moved on a long way, but Kawasaki's first liquid-cooled four played a big part in bringing that class about.

Not content with that, the 592cc (36cu in) GPZ600R arrived the following year, 1984. This was another first, though this time the new class was for supersports liquid-cooled 600s. This has since became the standard format for all-round sportsbikes that combine good performance (this GPZ produced 75bhp and could better 209km/h/130mph) with reasonable running costs. Honda soon responded with its highly competent CBR600, which has

dominated this class ever since. But Kawasaki was there first. Its answer was the more powerful, lighter GPX600, and the physically bigger ZZR600 which, at the time of writing, is still selling in reasonable numbers.

While the company was concentrating on getting its sportsbikes right, the monstrous Z1300 was still selling to a limited market. Launched in 1978, this 294kg (648lb) machine was one of three sixes at the time, the other two being the Honda CBX and Benelli Sei. It came at a time when the horsepower race was in full swing, when cubic capacity and sheer size seemed to be a priority over handling and rideability. It is tempting now to see the

ABOVE: The KR-1S, a highly tuned 250cc two-stroke for the road

BELOW: A 1998 VL1500 in the cruiser mould

Z1300 as a dinosaur; smooth and sophisticated it may have been, but in the opinion of some, the description 'dinosaur' is probably right.

If the Z1300 was a model of conspicuous excess, the GTR of 1986 was something very different. It was Kawasaki's attempt at a purpose-built tourer, with shaft-drive, standard fairing and panniers, big comfortable seat and a huge six-gallon fuel tank for those cross-Europe jaunts. Although it looked all-new, the GTR was really an intelligent mix of existing components with its frame based on that of the GPZ900 (with, of course, a Uni-Trak rear-end) and the engine a detuned version of the 997cc (61cu in)

liquid-cooled four from the GPZ1000RX. In GTR guise, the engine produced 108bhp, though it was restricted to 100bhp for some markets. Twelve years on, the GTR was still in production and had acquired a loyal following; Kawasaki's bid for a slice of the BMW market had worked well.

But the company had never forgotten its love affair with the ultimate big bike market which had begun with the Z1. The liquid-cooled GPZ1000RX had replaced the old air-cooled 1100, and was in turn dropped in favour of the faster ZX-10. Both of these led to something rather longer-lived and which made a much bigger impact – the ZZR1100. When it was launched in 1990, the ZZR1100 was simply the fastest

ABOVE: Kawasaki's Zephyr combined nineties technology with seventies style

production bike on sale (283km/h/176mph), a sports-tourer that handled very well indeed and really blurred the edges between the pure sports and sports-touring markets. Although it was developed from the ZX-10, the ZZR was also substantially new, with major changes to the engine with a new frame, bodywork and suspension. The bike's sheer zest and long legs which, for several years, made it the fastest one could buy, also made the ZZR1100 (always the ZX-11 in the U.S.) something of a cult motorcycle. Only in the late 1990s has it been overtaken in speed and power, but for some it is still the ultimate Japanese machine. In Britain, to members of the ZZR Owners Club, its slogan still holds

good: 'Nowhere's far on a ZZR!'

Fast the ZZR most certainly was, but it still weighed 233kg (514lb). For the pure sports market, Kawasaki needed a nimbler answer to Honda's all-conquering FireBlade, and unveiled it in 1994 as the ZX-9R, the first of the Ninja family. It was developed from the existing ZXR750, itself a more sporting development of the GPX750. Although it looked the part, and gave near-ZZR levels of performance, the original ZX was just too heavy and softly suspended to really challenge the FireBlade. Steady development and an almost complete redesign for 1998 brought it much closer to the top. The 599cc (36.5cu in) ZX6 was closer to the mark

straight away, with its own very compact and all-new power unit (98bhp at 12,600rpm) and aluminium frame. It certainly equalled the CBR600 on performance, though perhaps wasn't such an accomplished all-rounder. In 1996 the family was completed with the ZX7, which replaced the ZXR. This (like the ZXR had become) was as much a means of providing a competitive basis for 750cc Superbike racing as a road bike, something true of most 750 sportsters in the late 1990s.

But while the horsepower race continues, there was also a move in the nineties towards retro bikes. Whether it was part of a general nostalgia for past

times, or that most riders were now aged 40 or over and yearning for the bikes of their youth, the 1970s look was back. Kawasaki's contribution was the Zephyr, with air-cooled engine, no fairing, and distinctly 1970s styling. In 500, 550, 750 and 1100 forms, the Zephyr was quite a success. And if the roly-poly Zephyr was too laid-back, the ZRX1100 for 1997 echoed the café racer Z1-R, albeit with a detuned ZZR1100 engine. Or if one couldn't remember the seventies, Kawasaki's answer was the new GPZ1100 of 1995 which had a distinct family resemblance to the GPZ500 twin, but again used detuned ZZR1100 power. The Big K had come a long way from the B8 125.

CUSTOM CLASSIC

If you had the time and means to build the bike of your dreams, one that encompassed every idea you had, chances are you'd be disappointed if you built it. Why? Because Kawasaki has already done it for you.

Introducing the all-new 1991 Kawasaki Zephyr.

Created by the builders of the legendary Z-1 and GPz series, the Zephyr was conceived to fulfill the dreams of motorcyclists whose idea of the perfect machine is embodied in the clean, classic lines of bikes like the Z-1, but with the advantages of today's modern technology.

To start, we designed a double-cradle, high-tensile steel frame to create a low, lean chassis—one that's as nimble around town as it is on the bends.

Then we added a fork with rigid 39mm diameter stanchions and a pair of nitrogen-charged adjustable piggy-back-reservoir shocks that deliver riding

characteristics that will keep you satisfied for years to come.

For plenty of legendary Kawasaki performance, we bolted in a GPz-descended powerplant that's been specially updated to give a better power feeling in the low and middle ranges.

Semi-floating discs and dual-piston pin-slide calipers up front, and a strong disc brake on the back bring you to a stop with great "feel" and fade resistance.

Wide tyres grip the road for confidence-inspiring feel, while cast aluminium five-spoke wheels add to overall rigidity.

And from the luxurious chrome to the immaculate fit and finish, it's obvious Kawasaki paid attention to the small details that enthusiasts notice.

So take a ride on a Kawasaki Zephyr.

It's one classic that won't take long to appreciate.

- Proven 550cc In-Line Four packs plenty of reliable Kawasaki firepower.
- Digital electronic ignition provides the right spark at any rpm.
- From headers to muffler, the four-into-one exhaust system glistens in high-quality chrome.
- Six-speed gearbox features Kawasaki's convenient Positive Neutral Finder.
- Adjustable dual war nitrogen-charged shocks feature piggy-back reservoirs for consistent damping action and less fade.
- Aluminium swingarm features eccentric chain adjusters that turn a chore into a piece of cake.
- Semi-floating front discs and dual-piston calipers bring the Zephyr to strong, sure stops.
- Adjustable handlevers and retractable bungee-cord hooks are just some of the Zephyr's rider-friendly extras.
- One-piece saddle is roomy enough to keep you and a friend comfortable on long rides.
- Instrumentation is clean, simple, and tells you what you need to know at a glance.

1992 RANGE

Kawasaki

THE GREAT ESCAPE

GPz 305

Fun, fun, **affordable** fun! That's what sums up this twin-cylinder sports bike — but it is also highly practical, being capable of motorway cruising as well as back-roads fun.

The engine likes to rev and the six-speed gearbox lets you make full use of its potential. If you have a restricted budget but want a 'real' sports bike, then look no further!

Toothed belt final drive is long lasting, gives very smooth transmission and reduces maintenance to a minimum.

- ▶ Twin-cylinder 4-stroke engine
- ▶ No messy lubrication for toothed belt final drive
- ▶ Rising rate Uni-Trak rear suspension
- ▶ Lightweight, sports handling
- ▶ Exceptional value for money

Colours: Ebony
Firecraker Red

KLR 250

A really versatile machine powered by a liquid-cooled four-stroke engine with class-leading power thanks to liquid-cooling and a four-valve head. Very civilised and street-friendly with its dual counter-rotating balance shafts to dampen vibration.

Long travel suspension, good ground clearance and four-stroke pulling power makes the KLR250 a great off-road machine too, where the quiet exhaust note won't cause offence.

- ▶ 4-valve, liquid-cooled 4-stroke engine
- ▶ Dry weight just 118kg (260lbs)
- ▶ Long travel suspension (230mm) front and rear
- ▶ Kawasaki Automatic Compression Release (KACR) for easy starting
- ▶ Disc front brake complements rear drum

Colours: Polar White
Ebony

KR-1S

If the KR-1S looks like it has strayed from the race tracks, that is hardly surprising – for it has excelled in Production and Supersport 400 events.

In the heat of competition, the light, rigid chassis has proved its worth in providing superb handling, allowing rapid changes of direction in safety and liberating the (considerable) potential of the liquid-cooled twin-cylinder two-stroke engine.

But the KR-1S was designed first and foremost as a road machine, so it remains civilised, despite its obvious sporting potential. The electronically-operated Kawasaki Integrated Power-valve System (KIPS) significantly broadens the power band, while balance shafts effectively dampen vibration.

- ▶ Double box section alloy frame and strong swing arm give superb handling
- ▶ Super-rigid 41mm dia. front fork stanchions
- ▶ Remote reservoir rear shock absorber has adjustable preload and damping
- ▶ Twin semi-floating front disc brakes with 4-piston calipers
- ▶ Wide, low profile, radial ply tyres

Colours: Firecracker Red/Pearl Gentry Grey
Lime Green/Blue 24/Pearl Alpine White

47

GPZ1100 used a detuned ZZR engine in a cheaper package

KELLER *Switzerland 1930–32*
An ultimately unsuccessful 347cc (21cu in) sv single.

KEMPTON *England 1921–22*
Used an ABC 124cc (8cu in) ohv engine to power both lightweights and scooters.

KENI *Germany 1921–23*
145/158cc (9/10cu in) three-port two-strokes.

KENILWORTH *England 1919–24*
An advanced scooter with front and rear suspension and Norman, Villiers or JAP power.

KENZLER-WAVERLEY *U.S.A. 1910–14*
Produced own ohv singles and V-twins.

KERRY *England 1902–66*
Originally only lasted until 1914, using Kelecom, FN and finally Abingdon engines. The name was used again from 1960 to sell Italian mopeds.

KESTREL *England 1903*
Used 211cc (13cu in) Minerva and MMC engines.

KG *Germany 1919–32*
An advanced shaft-driven single, using first an ioe 503cc (31cu in), then an ohv 499cc. There were several owners: the Krieger brothers, Cito, Allright and Paul Henkel, but was in any case outdated by the late 1920s.

KIEFT *England 1955–57*
Rebadged Hercules scooters and lightweights for the British market.

KILEAR *Czechoslovakia 1924–26*
Own 247cc (15cu in) three-port two-stroke machines.

KINETIC *India 1972–*
A licence-built Vespa Ciao moped (sold as the Luna), later producing its own Minarelli/Morini-inspired two-strokes, and a licence-built 100cc (6cu in) Honda scooter from 1986.

KING *England 1901–07*
Used a wide variety of power units, among them De Dion, Minerva, MMC, Daw, Antoine and Sarolea.

KING-JAP *Germany 1928–31*
Built from mostly English parts, including the sv and ohv singles.

KINGSBURY *England 1919–23*
A brief dalliance with scooters and lightweights, with its own 261cc (16cu in) engine.

KINGSWAY *England 1921–23*
Motorcycles of simple design with 293cc (18cu in) sv JAP engines.

K&K *Germany 1924–25*
Built its own 170 and 289cc (10 and 18cu in) three-port two-strokes.

KLOTZ *Germany 1923–26*
Another in-house two-stroke of 246cc (15cu in).

KM *Germany 1924–26*
Limited production 142 and 159cc (9 and 10cu in) two-stroke machines.

KMB *Germany 1923–26*
4.2–6hp machines of its own design and manufacture.

KMS *Germany 1922–24*
Used own 196cc (12cu in) ohv single, and a bought-in Grade two-stroke.

KÖBO *Germany 1921–26*
A 276cc (17cu in) two-stroke from a maker of chains.

KOCH *Czechoslovakia 1934–35*
Advanced unit-construction 348cc (21cu in) ohc single from ex-Praga designer J.F. Koch.

KOEHLER-ESCOFFIER *France 1912–57*
Produced mostly ohc engines, including the only 996cc (61cu in) ohc V-twin of the 1920s. Also used ohc singles, both in-house and bought-in. After 1945, concentrated on Villiers-powered lightweights.

KOFA *Germany 1923–25*
Used bought-in 283cc (17cu in) two-strokes.

KOHOUT *Czechoslovakia 1904–06*
Used 2.5/2.75hp Minerva and Fafnir engines.

KOLIBRI *Germany 1923–30*
A 110cc (7cu in) clip-on.

KOMAR *Poland c.1958–68*
Brand-name for ZZR mopeds.

KOMET *Germany 1902–05*
One of the first makers of two-strokes in Germany, with licence-built Ixions.

KONDOR *Germany 1924–25*
Machines with Simplex two-strokes or an Ideal sv unit was offered.

KOSTER (KS) *Germany 1923–25*
Used a pressed steel frame, disc wheels, and enclosed belt/chain-drive. Bekamo or Cockerell-powered.

KOVROV *Former U.S.S.R. 1946–*
Like many others, it built a copy of the DKW RT125, soon increasing capacity to 175cc (11cu in). Also built the Voskhod from 1966 and a few 250cc (15cu in) motocrossers.

KR *Germany 1924–25*
Used the 492cc (30cu in) sv flat-twin BMW engine, or a 998cc (61cu in) MAG V-twin was available.

KR *Germany 1930–1933*
No connection with the above and using bought-in JAP singles.

KRAMMER *Austria 1926–29*
Used 172cc (10.5cu in) Villiers, 496cc (30cu in) ohv Anzani or MAG, or 996cc (61cu in) Anzani 8-valve V-twins.

KRASNY-OCTOBER *Former U.S.S.R. 1930–34*
First mass-produced bike from Soviet Russia, similar to the equivalent DKW.

KRAUSER *Germany 1976–*
As well as running the Kreidler racing team in later years, BMW dealer Mike Krauser built a limited run of tubular frames to take BMW engines, which were sold as kits or complete bikes.

KREIDLER *Germany 1951–82*
At one time the biggest manufacturer in Germany, despite concentrating solely on 49cc (3cu in) machines. The sporting Florett, with 6.25bhp, could top 85km/h (53mph) and was also very successful in 50cc racing, gaining several World Championships. Closed in 1982 due to falling sales.

KRIEGER *Germany 1925–26*
Used 347cc (21cu in) Blackburne engines, and the Krieger brothers' own 499cc (30cu in) shaft-driven singles (then owned by Allright). Also sold frames to other manufacturers.

Krauser reframed BMW twins to good effect

From the 1970s, KTM was increasingly dominated by the off-road market

KRS *Germany 1921–26*
Used Paqué four-stroke singles and the SWM-built Bosch-Douglas flat twin.

KRUPP *Germany 1919–21*
Scooter, with 185 or 198cc (11 or 12cu in) engine fitted outside the front wheel.

KSB *Germany 1924–29*
Fitted a variety of engines from DKW, Kühne, Blackburne and JAP.

KTM *Austria 1953–*
The most successful Austrian manufacturer began with 98cc (6cu in) Rotax-powered machines and went on to produce mopeds, scooters and lightweights with Puch, Sachs as well as Rotax engines, all two-strokes. KTM went through phases, concentrating solely on mopeds in 1960–65, and from 1967 began to develop motocross bikes which came to dominate its production. Won the 1977 250cc Motocross Championship, and experience gained from the competition bikes trickled down to the production machines, resulting in water-cooling and rising-rate rear suspension. After near-bankruptcy in 1991, KTM made a rapid recovery, and now produces a large range of off-road machines from a 125cc (8cu in) two-stroke trail bike to more serious Enduros (two-strokes of 193, 297 and 368cc/12, 18 and 22cu inches, and four-strokes of 398, 539 and 625cc/24, 33 and 38cu inches). Some of these are road-legal and have electric start. Another recent development has been a return to the pure road market with the LC4 Supermoto (basically the Enduro, but with road tyres and other minor changes) and the 625cc Duke, the magazine testers' favourite for wheelies and stoppies! Although there were

The Kymco Zing 125 cruiser

KTM four-stroke Pro-Lever 500 GS

rumours of a merger and takeover in 1998 (notably by Harley-Davidson) KTM remains independent in early 1999, is profitable, and is now developing its own V-twin.

KULI *Germany 1922–24*
145cc and 198cc (9 and 12cu in) two-strokes.

KUMFURT *England 1914–16*
Utilized 269cc or 496cc (16 or 30cu in) Precision V-twins.

KURIER *Germany 1921–24*
Used own 147cc (9cu in) two-strokes and also sold to other manufacturers.

KURRAS *Germany 1925–27*
Utilized 173cc (11cu in) water-cooled

Bekamo two-strokes in its own triangular frames. Not many were made.

KV *Germany 1924–27*
Produced 197cc and 246cc (12 and 15cu in) sv singles.

KYMCO *Taiwan 1962–*
A recent entry to the huge Taiwanese industry, at the time of writing, Kymco (short for Kwang Yang Motor Co.) is one of the largest scooter manufacturers in the world, and has achieved great success in Europe. Began with Japanese-derived 50cc (3cu in) scooters, but in the late 1990s offers a complete range of 50, 100 and 250cc scooters, both two- and four-strokes, plus a 125 (8cu in) cruiser-style motorcycle.

KYNOCH *England 1912–13*
Mainly used its own 488cc (30cu in) single and 770cc (47cu in) V-twin.

KZ *Germany 1924–25*
Utilized 198cc (12cu in) Alba engines, and ohv 348cc (21cu in) singles made by Kühne.

L

L-300 *Former U.S.S.R. 1932–*
Produced DKW-like 294/346cc (18/21cu in) two-strokes, built in large numbers for the military.

LABOR *France 1908–60*
Part of the Alcyon group, with 98–248cc (6–15cu in) two-strokes and 174–498cc (11–30cu in) four-strokes.

LADETTO *Italy 1923–32*
Produced 123/173cc (7.5/11cu in) two-strokes at first. The Ladetto brothers were later joined by Angelo Blatto, and built four-strokes.

Kymco Top Boy off-road-style scooter

LADIES PACER *England 1914*
Probably the only motorcycle ever built on the island of Guernsey, it had a step-through frame with a JES 110cc (7cu in) two-stroke.

LADY *Belgium 1925–38*
Used a variety of engines up to 498cc (30cu in), which included units from Villiers, MAG, Blackburne *et al.*

LAFOUR & NOUGIER *France 1927–36*
Aubier-Dunne, Chaise, Stainless, Train, Villiers and JAP supplied the power.

LAG *Austria 1921–29*
Produced 118/148cc (7/9cu in) clip-ons at first, later fitted JAP engines and designed its own 246cc (15cu in) two-stroke.

LA GALBAI *Italy 1921–25*
Own two-strokes from 276cc to 492cc (17 to 30cu in), the biggest of which was a V-twin.

LAGONDA *England 1902–05*
Mostly used De Dion, MMC or Minerva engines.

L'ALBA *Italy 1924–26*
Produced 198cc (12cu in) Alba sv machines, assembled in Milan.

LA LORRAINE *France 1922–25*
Built own two-stroke engines up to 248cc (15cu in).

LAMAUDIÈRE *France 1901–07*
Surely the biggest single ever made at 942cc (57cu in).

LAMBRETTA *Italy 1947–1971*
It can be no coincidence that the world's two most popular scooters both originated

Side and front views of the Lambretta A Model – simple, basic transport, and ideal for late 1940s Italy

in post-war Italy within a year of one another. That Vespa and Lambretta turned out to be so similar – and for a time equally successful – was no accident of history. Italy in the late 1940s desperately needed cheap, basic personal transport, but so did the rest of Europe. Germany had its own post-war scooter boom, but it was in Italy that scooters became part of the cultural scenery with the sound of buzzing two-strokes filling the streets of every town and city. Whether it was climate, or Italian flair, or even those crowded cities with narrow streets, scooters seemed to suit Italy. So where scooter manufacturers in Germany, Britain or France went back to motorcycles, or gave up altogether, the Vespa and Lambretta went on to achieve

huge worldwide success, being built under licence all over the globe. If one includes three-wheelers, 24 million Lambrettas have been built over the years.

Ferdinando Innocenti had no ambition to build scooters, but he was a talented engineer and possessed of great energy and drive. He opened his own small workshop at the age of 18 and began experimenting with the application of steel tubes. He moved to Rome, then Milan, where in 1931 he set up a plant to mass-produce his steel tubes. It was a great success and grew into a huge factory until Allied bombing heavily damaged it in World War II. Undaunted, he set about the task of reconstruction and typically succeeded before the end of the war.

History does not record what gave him the idea for a scooter, but the Lambretta (named after the Lambrate area of Milan) was an ideal way to diversify. It was a simple thing with a pressed steel main-frame and a rear sub-frame to carry the engine made of (you've guessed it) steel tubes. The engine itself was a 123cc (7.5) two-stroke, coupled to a three-speed gearbox and with foot change, though the famous twistgrip change was to come the following year. With 4.1hp at 4,500rpm, it could push the A Model along at 64–71km/h (40–44mph), and at a 48km/h (30mph) cruise sipped fuel at around 39km per litre (110mpg). There was no rear suspension on this first Lambretta, but luckily the tiny (7-inch) tyres were like

The Lambretta Model B gained rear suspension and longer wheels, though it was still not the ideal sidecar machine!

The Lambretta 50cc (3cu in) J Model, whose familiar style was by now well-established

LD150LC introduced full bodywork

ABOVE: The TV175 was the biggest yet

BELOW: The Series III 150, four-speed with 10-inch wheels

low-pressure balloons that no doubt softened the ride. Available in several colours, plus a dash of chrome, the Lambretta A was a great success, and over 9,000 were sold in the first year.

However, Innocenti soon learned from this experience, and the B Model of late 1948 had rear suspension, slightly larger 8-inch wheels and the twistgrip gearchange. And the cables now ran outside the handlebars, which didn't look as neat but were a lot easier to manipulate. It cost more than the A, but Innocenti was obviously moving in the right direction as 35,000 were sold in just 13 months. But things were moving fast, and February 1950 saw the C model, whose main innovation was the large single-tube frame which has formed the basis of every Lambretta since. It was described as a 'sports model' (presumably because it did

without leg guards, though in reality was no faster than the earlier bikes).

Full Enclosure

But none of these Lambrettas resembled the classic Italian scooter that we all recognize. That came in April 1950 with the 125LC. Mechanically, there was little change, with the same mildly tuned 123cc single. What was new was the full bodywork with leg guards right up to the handlebars, full enclosure for the engine, and proper footboards for both rider and passenger. (From the start, all Lambrettas had room for two, for what self-respecting young Italian could be expected to ride solo?) This didn't mean the end of the basic open Lambretta, though, and these were produced right up to 1956. But the future of the scooter lay in full weather protection and a 150cc (9.2cu in) version of both soon appeared, now with fan cooling thanks to blades on the flywheel. With 6hp, the Lambretta could top 80km/h (50mph) on a good day, and came in both open and enclosed versions.

The LD was now the mainstream Lambretta, with a 125 or 150cc engine and leading link front suspension. One innovation, which appeared in February 1954, was an electric start version which utilized a 6-volt battery hidden behind the left-hand panel, though it was soon uprated to 12 volts. At the time, however, it seems to have been less popular than the simpler, cheaper kickstart model. But the basic Lambrettas were selling better than ever and the Series III 150LD sold over 100,000 in 18 months which was partly due to rapidly expanding exports. In 1948, just 96 Lambrettas had been sold outside Italy: ten years on, the figure was 109,000. For many developing countries, the Lambretta was ideal transport, but too expensive to import fully-built. The best solution was to build it under licence, thereby creating jobs and skills at home. Factories were set up in India (where Lambrettas are still made) and in various parts of South America, Indonesia and Pakistan, among other locations.

Meanwhile, Europeans had the updated LI range with shaft-drive, larger 10-inch wheels and four-speed twistgrip. Engine power was slightly up, though the basic unit was still a 123c two-stroke. But the new top of the range scooter had already appeared, the 170cc (10.4cu in) TV175. With 8.6hp, it promised 103km/h (64mph) and a mere 31km per litre (88mpg) and it even had a front disc brake! Unfortunately, engine problems led to its replacement by a Series

ABOVE: GP125 was the final update

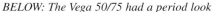

II in 1959, which was slower but more reliable. But export markets (notably British) wanted still more power, and Lambretta's response was the TV200 of 1963. It had the same basic underpinnings as every other Lambretta (apart from that front disc brake), albeit with a 10.75hp 198cc (12cu in) engine. Top speed was 97km/h (60mph). By 1966, it had become the SX200, with 11hp and a claimed 106km/h (66mph), yet according to Innocenti could still manage 33km per litre (93mpg). Inevitably, the British importer coined the advertising slogan 'SX Appeal'.

In the late sixties, Lambretta also attempted to branch out from its traditional scooters into various mopeds; these were boosted by Italian legislation which treated 50s as bicycles. There were very basic big-wheel mopeds in the 1950s, but the Vega (in 50 and 75cc/3 and 4.6cu inch forms) looked like a miniaturized, space-age Lambretta scooter, and was in production from 1968–70. 50cc versions of the scooters appeared from 1964 on, as the three-speed J50, which lasted right up to the end of production in 1971.

The more basic Lambrettas had another update in January 1969 with the Grand Prix (GP), which featured styling by the famous Bertone design house, though it was very obviously still a Lambretta. Rather than attempt anything too radical, Bertone had simply updated the basic lines, which was probably wise. Still, the period racing stripe was distinctive and the GP125, 150 and 200 carried on until April 1971. For the Italian factory this was the end, as sales were well past their peak and Innocenti had other projects to pursue. But as we have seen, Lambretta lives on all over the world.

BELOW: The Vega 50/75 had a period look

SX200 was Lambretta's top-range scooter in 1966 and could top 106km/h (66mph)

LA MONDIALE *Belgium 1924–33*
No connection with the Italian Mondial, 308/349cc (19/21cu in) two-strokes or bigger ohc Chaise engines were used in pressed steel frames. There were also Villers and JAP options.

LAMPO *Italy 1925–27*
123–247cc (7.5–15cu in) two-stroke lightweights, also offered with the 173cc (10.5) ohv Piazza unit.

LANCER *Japan 1957–early 1960s*
Two-strokes up to 248cc (15cu in) and a 248cc V-twin like the more famous Lilac.

LANCO *Austria 1922–26*
Used MAG engines at first before utilizing its own 496cc (30cu in) singles.

LANDI *Italy 1923–26*
Produced 122/172cc (7.4/10.5cu in) three-port two-strokes.

LA PANTHERRE *France 1928–32*
Utilized 346/490cc (21/30cu in) JAP singles.

LAPIZE *France 1930–37*
Used Aubier-Dunne, LMP, JAP and other bought-in units.

LATSCHA *France 1948–53*
Only used Aubier-Dunne two-strokes.

LAURIN & KLEMENT *Austria 1899–1908*
One of the leading pioneer motorcycle factories in the early years, Laurin & Klement produced singles, V-twins and even four-cylinder in-line four machines.

There were some innovations, notably water-cooling and, on the CC V-twin, front suspension. Concentrated on cars from 1908, and was later taken over by Skoda.

L'AVENIR *Belgium 1959*
Used HMW and Sachs 49cc (3cu in) engines.

LAVERDA *Italy 1949–*
Pietro Laverda never built motorcycles, but then his business lay in agricultural machinery. He set up a factory to build ploughs and harrows in Breganze in north-eastern Italy in 1873 and it grew into an industrial group, still owned by the Laverda family. But it wasn't until 1948, two generations later, that Francesco Laverda built his first bike, a 75cc (4.6cu in) four-stroke. It was really for his own amusement, but so many friends asked him to build replicas that he set up Moto Laverda the following year and went into production. He had a distinct advantage in that he had a background of engineering resources and plenty of capital, and the little 75cc ohv single was made by the fledgling company itself, hanging the bike from a pressed steel frame. Despite the small capacity, this was no utility bike but a true miniaturized sportster, a fact which was underlined in 1953 when an example won its class in the 1,127-km (700-mile) Milan–Taranto road race. Other long-distance races like the Giro d'Italia were contested, encouraging Laverda to design a larger bike.

A 100cc (6cu in) racer followed, and there were more basic bikes as well, such as a moped (albeit with a front disc brake) and a four-stroke scooter. In fact, at this

time Laverda was as much concerned with utility bikes as anything else, which belied its later association with powerful road-burners. Take the 200cc (12cu in) Gemini, announced in 1960. This still used a pressed steel frame to house its 11bhp twin-cylinder four-stroke engine. It was high geared for quiet cruising, had a large comfortable dual seat, enclosed chain and a useful luggage rack. Leg guards were among the options, and when the American magazine *Cycle World* tested one in 1967, it found that the top speed was an underwhelming 84km/h (52mph). If Laverda had gone on building bikes like this in the face of nippier Japanese lightweights, it surely would not have lasted far into the 1970s.

A Big Leap
Fortunately, the company had something radically different up its sleeve. Radically different, that is, compared to what it had built before. Not so radical by Honda standards, for Laverda's new 650cc (40cu in) twin, announced in late 1966, had much in common (in both looks and general layout) with Honda's CB450. As unveiled, there was something of a Honda about the whole bike. Still, none of that seemed to matter because wherever the inspiration had come from, Laverda had evidently done a good job. The sohc twin, with 360-degree crankshaft and five-speed gearbox, produced 52bhp at 6,500rpm for a claimed top speed of 190km/h (118mph). Just as important, Laverda claimed that it was designed to run at least 60,000 miles before major overhaul, the crankshaft being supported by massive ball and roller bearings. Here was a thoroughly modern

ABOVE and OPPOSITE: The Laverda 1000 triple was the first of a generation

update of the vertical twin, with competitive power, long-distance stamina and such niceties as electric start. This surely was what the British industry should have been building at the time and it was instructive that contemporary British twins of the same capacity should be plagued with vibration, while Laverda was not, neither was it over-tuned.

At the behest of the importers, the 650 quickly became a 750 for the bike's U.S. launch, and in this guise the 744cc (45cu in) American Eagle, as it was known, pushed out 60bhp at 6,500rpm, still on a very modest compression ratio of 7.0:1 and with mild tuning for a tractable, torquey engine. Tests praised the performance, quality and handling, only finding it a little heavy in town (it weighed well over 227kg/500lb). In the space of a couple of years, Laverda had transformed itself from an obscure maker of decidedly Italianate lightweights to mainstream sportsbikes in the up and coming 750 class.

T. Parker riding a 750cc (46cu in) Laverda SFC at Brands Hatch

looked very much like a three-cylinder version of the twin, but the production engine of 1972 was neater, more compact, with twin overhead camshafts and a claimed 80bhp. Apart from Triumph, no one was making a four-stroke triple at the time, so it showed courage on Laverda's part. There was still much of the twin about it, with a strong bottom-end and an initial tune aiming at mid-range rather than top-end power, yet top speed was over 209km/h (130mph) and it completed the standard quarter-mile in less than 14 seconds. Perhaps most surprising, after the somewhat heavy 750, was the fact that road testers found the big bike lighter and easy to handle and at 214kg (471lb), it actually *was* lighter. On the other hand, the stiff suspension, high first gear and heavy clutch ('requires a fine, manly grip', said *Cycle*) made it clear that this was a bike intended for the open road.

The triple may have been a great success, and turned out to be Laverda's most enduring model, but there were some failures, notably the Zündapp-powered two-stroke road bikes of 125 and 175cc (8 and 11cu in). The later 125/250 Enduros, this time using Husqvarna units, were similarly unsuccessful, though Laverda had earlier designed its own 250/400cc (15/24cu in) two-stroke Enduro. The company evidently had ambitions to build smaller bikes again, for 1977 saw the launch of the Alpino 500, a slim and lightweight vertical twin whose looks (engine-wise) reminded one of the first 650, except this one had twin overhead cams and four valves per cylinder. Power was 44bhp at 8,000rpm. Although more expensive than the Japanese opposition, it certainly handled well, and was just as fast

Inevitably, with such a mildly tuned standard machine, a sportster (the SF) soon appeared, with a higher 8.9:1 compression and other changes for 65bhp at 7,500rpm, and a top speed of near 193km/h (120mph). The softer original continued as the GT, but that wasn't all as the SFC ('Super Freni Competiziono') from 1971 again had higher tune, with bigger valves and fiercer profile cams.

Bottom-end components were polished, and the pistons were balanced in matched pairs. Power was up to 70bhp, later 75bhp. It was really designed for Production Racing, though was fully road-legal with lights and silencers. It certainly fulfilled its promise, taking the top three places in the Barcelona 24-hour Endurance race in 1971, not to mention wins at Vallelunga, Modena and Zeltweg the following year,

and the Zandvoort 6-hour in 1973.

But in those days, Moto Laverda was not a company to rest on its laurels, particularly with brothers Massimo and Pietro Laverda on the Board. Both were keen riders and realized that good though the twin was, it would soon be outclassed by ever bigger and faster fours from Japan. The three-cylinder 1000 was their response. When first revealed to the press in 1970, it

The Laverda 500cc (30.5cu in) Alpina was an attempt to meet the Japanese head-on

at 167km/h (104mph). The Alpino lasted until 1981, by which time it was supplemented by the 52bhp café racer-style Montjuic. In its final form, as the 500T/S from 1982–84, it had a balance shaft and was a little more sophisticated. In the final analysis, though, none of Laverda's 500s were sufficiently different to the opposition, not in the way that the bigger bikes were.

The Jota

Meanwhile, Laverda's most famous bike of all time had been launched in 1976. The U.K. importer, Roger Slater, just like Laverda's U.S. importer a decade earlier, had persuaded the factory to produce something faster. The result was the Jota. It was the basic triple, with high-compression pistons, sharper cams and freer-breathing exhausts to produce 90bhp

or so, and a top speed of 225km/h/140mph (some said 150mph). There were now twin disc brakes at the front too, which was probably just as well. Despite the higher state of tune, in the Laverda tradition it remained strong on torque and mid-range power. It was one of the fastest things on the road at the time, and the low-set bars emphasized the fact that this was the sports version. It also served to take over

where the SFC left off, and Production Racing success once more fell to Laverda.

As was the way with legends, it became diluted over the years, notably after Laverda made it smoother with a 120-degree crankshaft (this was in pre-balance-shaft days) and a little easier to ride. It was supplanted by the 1115cc (68cu in) Mirage in 1980, which had even more mid-range power but was otherwise little advanced on the original 981cc (60cu in) triple. In 1982 came the more civilized RGS, with a half-fairing, hydraulic clutch and the 120-degree engine, though it only lasted a couple of years, as did the tuned 241km/h (150mph) Corsa version, and the naked RGA. But Laverda knew that the air-cooled triple was coming to the end of its useful life, and in 1983 work was progressing on a water-cooled four to replace it. This was not a clean-sheet design, but owed much to the abortive V6 Endurance racer of the late seventies. The V6 was a real departure for Laverda: it not only had a water-cooled engine, but four valves per cylinder, shaft-drive and electronic ignition. Only six months after work began, an engine was running and producing 118bhp at the rear wheel, well on the way to the 140bhp target. Designed solely with Endurance racing in mind, the bike enjoyed a wide spread of power but was heavy. It had just one outing, at the 1978 Bol d'Or, where it retired after eight and a half hours, due to a broken driveshaft joint. Despite stunning speed (at 282km/h/175mph on the Mistral straight, it was 18mph faster than the works Hondas) it never raced again.

The V6 had also cost a great deal of money to develop, and work on other

Laverda's softly-tuned GTL750, seen here in Basano, was popular with the Italian police

ABOVE: Laverda Mirage 1200   *BELOW: Laverda 750 SF*

ABOVE: The Laverda 750S of 1997 served a specialized sports market

projects in the early 1980s also swallowed capital, notably a 600/750cc (37/45cu in) triple that was based on half the V6, and a V3 two-stroke 350 that reached prototype form but ran into pollution and fuel consumption problems. Instead, the new owner (Prinefi, a Milan-based investment house) authorized work on an eight-valve V-twin, though this too came to nothing. Meanwhile, a 125cc two-stroke and 600cc twin-cylinder trail bike carried on. It wasn't until 1992 that the bike that would finally get Laverda properly up and running again appeared. It was an oil-cooled 668cc (41cu in) vertical twin, with Weber/Marelli fuel injection and around 70bhp at around 8,900rpm. Although not as powerful as the Japanese supersport 600s, the 650 did push Laverda back into the performance market. It was replaced by the 668 in 1996, basically the same bike, but with a broader spread of power, and joined by the naked Ghost. The following year came the substantially new water-cooled 750 twin, with 78bhp or 92bhp, and this machine takes Laverda through to the year 2000.

The man behind this new impetus was textile tycoon Francesco Tognon, who had taken over the company and injected fresh capital in 1994. There was talk of a successor to the original triple (water-cooled this time) for launch in September 1998. However, Laverda was no stranger to the company politics which had long been a part of the Italian bike industry. In early 1998, Tognon sold a part-share in the company to the Spezzapria brothers before later in the year departing to pursue other interests. All this delayed the new Jota, as it was known, but the company was confident of a September 1999 launch. In the meantime, a long-stroke version of the 750 twin, the 800TTS, was displayed at the October 1998 Munich Show, and is promised for production by the middle of 1999. All this was thrown into doubt in January 1999, when Francesco Tognon left to take over Bimota. Now in majority control, the Spezzapria brothers have revealed a prototype of the 899cc 135bhp water-cooled triple to attract new investment from outside. If that investment materializes, the reborn Laverda will be building on quite a legacy.

LAZZATI *Italy 1899–1904*
One of Italy's first manufacturers, it used De Dion engines.

L&C *England c.1904*
Fitted De Dion, Minerva and Antoine engines.

LDR *Germany 1922–25*
Produced its own 548cc (33cu in) sv single, with external flywheel.

The V6 racer with Massimo Laverda (left) – heavy but powerful

LEFT and ABOVE: The water-cooled Laverda V6 was designed for Endurance racing

LEA FRANCIS *England 1911–26*
Used JAP or MAG engines, usually V-twins. The famous writer and dramatist George Bernard Shaw rode one.

LECCE *Italy 1930–32*
Used 173cc (11cu in) ohv Moser engines, but with a modified valve layout.

LE FRANÇAIS-DIAMANT *France 1912–59*
Alcyon-owned, it built 98–498cc (6–30cu in) machines and, after 1945, small two-strokes only.

LEGNANO *Italy 1932–68*
First built under the Wolsit name and after

the war made Garelli, Sachs or Mosquito-engined mopeds.

LE GRIMPEUR *France c.1900–32*
Produced a variety of machines from 98cc (6cu in) two-strokes to big V-twins with engines by MAG, JAP, Aubier-Dunne, Stainless, Chaise, etc.

LELIOR *France 1922–24*
A 174cc (11cu in) flat twin and 246cc (15cu in) single, both two-strokes.

LEM *Italy 1974*
Used Minarelli and Franco-Morini engines in mopeds and children's bikes.

LEONARD *England 1903–06*
Used Minerva, MMC and Fafnir engines.

LEONARDO FRERA *Italy 1930–34*
Used 173–346cc (11–21cu in) sv and ohv singles from JAP.

LEOPARD *Germany 1921–26*
Built own engines, both 248/346cc (15/21cu in) two-strokes and ohc singles.

LEPROTTO *Italy 1951–54*
Produced its own ohv singles of 123–198cc (7.5–12cu in) capacity.

LETHBRIDGE *England 1922–23*
Utilized 247 or 269cc (15 or 16cu in) Villiers power.

LETO *Germany 1926–28*
The pressed steel frame incorporated the fuel tank, with Rinne two-stroke engines.

LE VACK *England 1923*
A 346cc (21cu in) JAP-engined machine, built by famous rider Herbert (Bert) Le Vack.

LEVIS *England 1911–40*
A leading producer of two-strokes, conventional 211/245cc (13/15cu in) singles, as well as a six-port version and prototype flat twin. Produced ohv and ohc four-stroke singles as well.

LFG *Germany 1921–25*
The 163cc (10cu in) four-stroke powered wheel could be fitted to any bicycle. Odder was the 305cc (19cu in) two-stroke motorcycle with airship-like body.

LGC *England 1926–32*
A Villiers- or JAP-engined sportster.

ABOVE: *A 1932 350 Levis*

BELOW: *Lilac produced upmarket lightweights*

LIAUDOIS *France 1923–27*
Used Train two-strokes of 98–173cc (6–11cu in).

LIBERATOR *France 1902–c.1929*
Used mainly Antoine, Sarolea and JAP engines.

LIBERIA *France 1920–65*
98–248cc (6–15cu in) Aubier-Dunne-powered two-strokes.

LILAC *Japan 1949–67*
One of the longer-lived Japanese marques, Lilac began with a simple 148cc (9cu in) four-stroke, but soon went upmarket with a successful shaft-driven 90cc (5.5cu in) single, following it with a 339cc (21cu in) flat twin in 1954 and a 247cc (15cu in) V-twin in 1959, all shaft-driven. There was a 493cc (30cu in) flat twin from 1964.

LILIPUT *Germany 1923–26*
Used Namapo, DKW, Baumi, Gruhn and other bought-in engines.

LILLIPUT *Italy 1899–c.1906*
Produced one horsepower (285cc/17cu in) engines.

LILY *England 1906–14*
Used Minerva, Villers or T.D. Cross units to 499cc (30cu in).

LINCOLN-ELK *England 1902–24*
Used own sv singles designed by James Kirby, with a V-twin after World War I.

LINER *Japan 1955–56*
Another upmarket shaft-driven Japanese bike of up to 246cc (15cu in). Like Lilac

and Honda, the company learned to concentrate on the bikes that made most money for the company.

LINSER *Austria 1904–10*
Produced its own 492cc (30cu in) singles and 618cc (38cu in) V-twins. Also known under the Zeus name.

LINSNER *Germany 1922–24*
All flat twins, with Bosch-Douglas or early BMW power.

LINX *Italy 1929–1941*
Used 173–598cc (11–36cu in) singles from Blackburne, Piazza, JAP and there was also a four-valve Python.

LION-RAPIDE *Belgium 1936–53*
Used Villiers, Ilo and FN singles up to 347cc (21cu in).

LITTLE GIANT *England 1913–15*
225cc (14cu in) two-strokes and 199cc (12cu in) sv singles.

LLOYD *England 1903–23*
Heavy sidevalves, with own 499cc (30cu in) singles and 842cc (51cu in) V-twins.

LLOYD *Germany 1922–26*
Its sole model was a 144cc (9cu in) two-stroke.

LLOYD *Germany 1923–26*
A 137cc (8cu in) clip-on, then JAP-engined mid-size bikes using many English parts.

LLOYD *The Netherlands 1930–31*
Bought in both its engines (DKW) and most of the pressed steel frame (Hulla).

LMP *France 1921–31*
Produced two- and four-strokes of up to 497cc (30cu in).

LMS *Germany 1923*
Another ex-airship builder which, like its compatriot LFG, attempted to apply airship-shaped bodies to motorcycles. Not many were made.

LOCOMOTIEF *The Netherlands 1952–66*
Pluvier and Sachs-powered mopeds.

LOHNER *Austria 1950–58*
Made scooters with Sachs or Ilo two-stroke power.

LOMOS *Germany 1922–24*
Early scooter with a pressed steel frame made by DKW and later by Eichler. Used a DKW two-stroke engine of 142cc (9cu in).

LONDON *England c.1903*
De Dion, Minerva and MMC engine power.

LORD *Germany 1929–31*
Used a 198cc (12cu in) JAP sv engine.

LORENZ *Germany 1921–1922*
A short-lived early scooter of 211cc (13cu in).

LORENZ *Germany 1921–25*
Perhaps the only twin-cylinder clip-on, a 126cc (8cu in) flat twin on in-house frame.

LOT *Poland 1937*
Advanced 346cc (21cu in) two-stroke with unit-construction and shaft-drive.

LOUIS CLÉMENT *France 1920–32*
Produced its own 598/996cc (36/61cu in) ohc V-twins, but a 98cc (6cu in) two-stroke only from 1928.

LOUIS JANIOR *France 1921–24*
A 499cc (30cu in) sv flat twin.

LUBE *Spain 1949–65*
Used NSU two- and four-strokes up to 249cc (15cu in), then its own two-strokes when NSU closed.

LUCAS *Germany 1923–24*
First utilized a Bekamo two-stroke, then its own 148cc (9cu in) ohv single.

LUCER *France 1953–56*
Used a 173cc (11cu in) AMC ohv, or Aubier-Dunne two-strokes.

LUCIFER *France 1928–56*
Bought-in engines from Train, MAG and Chaise.

LUDOLPH *Germany 1924–26*
Designed its own two-strokes of up to 299cc (18cu in).

LUGTON *England 1912–14*
Used 498cc (30cu in) Precision or JAP engines.

LUJAN *Argentina 1946*
Used various brand names for its sub-125cc (8cu in) lightweights, some licence-built from Malaguti.

LUPUS *Germany 1923–26*
Its sole model was its own 148cc (9cu in) two-stroke.

LUTÈCE *France 1921–26*
Some of the few French big bikes, they were large vertical twins of 997 and 1016cc (61 and 62cu in), with shaft-drive.

LUTRAU *Germany 1924–33*
Built its own two-strokes of 198–346cc (12–21cu in), and also a 497cc (30cu in) sv single.

LUTZ *Germany 1949–54*
Mostly produced 49cc (3cu in) scooters and mopeds, though there was also a 173cc (11cu in) scooter.

LUWE *Germany 1924–28*
Bought-in engines from Paqué, JAP, MAG and Blackburne.

LWD *Germany 1923–26*
In-house 197/247cc (12/15cu in) sv singles.

M

MABECO *Germany 1923–27*
Actually a copy of the Indian Scout, with engines supplied by Max Bernhardt & Co. of Berlin (596cc and 749cc/36 and 46cu inch sv V-twins). From 1925 there was a 728cc (44cu in) ohv version.

MABON *England c.1905*
Used MMC, Fafnir and its own engines.

MABRET *Germany 1927–28*
Used only Kühne engines, both 346cc and 496cc (21 and 30cu in).

MACKLUM *England 1920–22*
2.5hp Peco two-strokes were used in this scooter-like machine.

MACO *Germany 1921–26*
Used own engines as well as DKWs.

MACQUET *France 1951–54*
Produced a 125cc (8cu in) clip-on.

MAFA *Germany 1923–27*
Used 119–246cc (7–15cu in) DKW and 348/496cc (21/30cu in) Kühne units.

MAFALDA *Italy 1923–28*
Built own three-port two-strokes to 173cc (11cu in).

MAFFEIS *Italy 1903–35*
First used a 2.25hp Sarolea, then designed its own singles and V-twins before finally using Blackburne engines. The Maffeis brothers raced their own bikes.

MAGATY *France 1931–37*
98cc (6cu in) two-strokes, powered by Train and Stainless units.

MAGDA *France 1933–36*
98/123cc (6/7.5cu in) two-strokes.

MAGNAT-DEBON *France 1906–58*
Started with Moser and Moto-Rêve singles and V-twins before designing its own engines after World War I. It was taken over by Terrot in 1924, and thereafter was used as a badge only. The Magnat-Moser subsidiary at Genoble used a V-twin Moser only.

MAGNEET *The Netherlands 1950s–early 1970s*
Moped maker, mainly using Sachs power.

MAGNET *Germany 1901–24*
Built own ioe and sv engines, including a 4.5hp V-twin.

ABOVE: *An early post-war Maico*   BELOW: *A 420cc (26cu in) motocrosser*

MAGNI *Italy 1928–30*
An ohc 348cc (21cu in) twin and 498cc (30cu in) single.

MAICO *Germany 1926–83*
Began with mopeds and lightweights fitted with 98/123cc (6/7.5cu in) Sachs and Ilo engines. Switched to making aircraft parts in the 1930s, and resumed motorcycle production in 1948 with its own 123cc two-stroke. Was soon offering a full range of small/mid-sized bikes including the fully-faired Maico-Mobil and Maicoletta touring scooter. From the late 1950s concentrated increasingly on off-road competition, which underpinned its fortunes right to the end. It built two-stroke motocross and enduro bikes.
OPPOSITE: *Maicos won World Motocross Championships*

ABOVE: A Maico two-stroke scrambler

and won the Manufacturers World Championship, though continued to build road bikes (both singles and twins) right through to the early 1980s. The motocrossers developed bigger engines (including a 48bhp 501cc) with water-cooling, disc-valves and trailing link forks. Maico went bankrupt in 1983 which spelt the end of all production, though another company bought the name.

MAINO *Italy 1902–56*
Intermittent production, but used 2.25hp Souverain engines and Sachs and NSU power after 1945.

MAJESTIC *France 1927–34*
Used Train, Chaise and JAP engines and was notable for a 498cc (30cu in) four-cylinder bike with full bodywork, car-like chassis and rear suspension.

MAJESTIC *Belgium 1928–31*
Made from English components, this machine was fitted with 346cc and 490cc (21 and 30cu in) single-cylinder sv and ohv JAP engines, with Burman gearboxes and other proprietory parts.

MAJESTIC *England 1931–35*
When the London-based Collier brothers of Matchless fame bought AJS, the parts department was bought by Ernie Humphries, boss of OK-Supreme of Birmingham. He built slightly modified AJS bikes and called them Majestics, most versions having 348cc and 498cc (21 and 30cu in) ohv engines.

MAJOR *Italy 1947–48*
Own 347cc (21cu in) engine, fully enclosed with shaft-drive.

MALAGUTI *Italy 1945–*
First mopeds used 38cc (2.3cu in) Garelli Mosquito engines, then units from Sachs and Franco-Morini. It still concentrates on mopeds and scooters, now up to 100cc (6cu in), both air- and water-cooled, notably the retro-styled Yesterday.

MALANCA *Italy 1956–86*
124/149cc (8/9cu in) two-stroke twins, as well as mopeds.

MAMMUT *Germany 1925–33*
Built Coventry-Eagle pressed steel frames under licence, with own two-strokes, and also used Villiers, Baumi and Blackburne engines.

MAMMUT *Germany 1953–56*
No connection to the above. Used Sachs and Ilo engines of 49–198cc (3–6cu in).

MAMOF *Germany 1922–24*
DKW and Grade-powered two-strokes, plus own 155cc (9.5cu in) sv single.

MANET *Czechoslovakia 1948–67*
Produced an 89cc (5.4cu in) double-pistoned two-stroke single, later 123cc (7.5cu in) scooters.

MANON *France 1903–c.1906*
Own 1.5hp engines.

MANTOVANI *Italy 1902–10*
1.5–4hp machines, some of which were in-house and water-cooled.

MANUFRANCE *France 1951–55*
Lightweights and scooters with 124/174cc (8/11cu in) engines.

MANURHIN *France 1955–62*
Took over production of the Hobby scooter after DKW dropped it.

MARC *France 1926–51*
Unremarkable bikes with Staub-JAP and LMP engines.

MARCK *Belgium 1904–08*
499cc (30cu in) ioe singles.

MARIANI *Italy 1930–34*
Made a 486cc (30cu in) single in two-valve form for the road, or with three valves if one chose to run it on naptha.

MARINI *Italy 1924–28*
124cc (8cu in) two-strokes.

MARLOE *England 1920–22*
Step-through frames with Precision or Blackburne engines.

MARLOW *England 1920–22*
346cc and 409cc (21 and 25cu in) JAP-engined machines, built to order.

MARMONNIER *France 1947–51*
Usually came supplied with Aubier-Dunne engines.

MARS (MA) *Germany 1903–57*
Built Fafnir and Zedel-engined bikes before World War I, but was most famous for the 986cc (60cu in) white Mars of 1920. The big flat-twin engine was supplied by Maybach and there was a two-speed gearbox and leg guards. German inflation killed it, but Mars was revived as MA with a variety of bought-in engines, concentrating in the 1930s on Sachs-powered mopeds and clip-ons. It used Sachs engines of up to 198cc/12cu inches up to the end for its well-made lightweights and mopeds.

MARS *England 1905–08*
Fitted Fafnir engines (as did the German Mars company) as well as the 211cc (13cu in) Minerva unit.

MARS *England 1923–26*
Used a variety of engines such as Bradshaws, Barr & Strouds and the inevitable Villiers.

MARSH *U.S.A. 1901–06*
Built its own singles and V-twins and was later known as MM.

MARSEEL *England 1920–21*
A 232cc (14cu in) scooter.

MARTIN *England 1911–22*
Fitted Precision and JAP engines to 498cc (30cu in).

MARTIN *Japan 1956–61*
Used bought-in two-strokes of 124–246cc (8–15cu in).

MARTINA *Italy 1924–57*
Built own 173cc (11cu in) two-strokes.

MARTINSHAW *England 1923–24*
Limited production using the Bradshaw 346cc (21cu in) single.

MARTINSYDE *England 1919–25*
Had its own range of ioe singles and V-twins of 346cc to 676cc (21 to 41cu in). When it closed, BAT bought what was left.

MARUSHO *Japan 1964–67*
A rebadged Lilac 493cc (30cu in) flat twin for the U.S. market. It had poor sales.

MARVEL *U.S.A. 1910–13*
Used Curtiss single-cylinder and V-twin engines.

MAS *Italy 1920–56*
Designed and built its own engines until the last few years, starting with small four-strokes which grew to 498cc (30cu in) during the 1930s. A modern 492cc vertical twin was added, as well as the Lupatta, MAS's first two-stroke. After the war, the 122cc (7.4cu in) Stella Alpina and ohc vertical twin were unsuccessful, though the company did better with the 173cc (11cu in) ohv Zenith and a Sachs-powered mini-scooter.

MAS *Germany 1923–24*
A 183cc (11cu in) two-stroke.

MASCOTTE *France 1923–24*
A 174cc (11cu in) sv lightweight.

MASERATI *Italy 1953–61*
Maserati's bikes never achieved the fame of its cars but a 123cc (7.5cu in) two-stroke and an ohc 248cc (15cu in) vertical twin were produced.

MASON & BROWN *England 1904–c.1908*
Used De Dion, Antoine, but mainly the 2hp Minerva engine.

MASSEY *England 1920–31*
Lightweights up to 490cc (30cu in). E.J. Massey also designed the first HRDs.

MAT *Czechoslovakia 1929–30*
Produced the 498cc (30cu in) Votroubek, similar to the Ariel Square Four but sv, with shaft-drive.

MATADOR *Germany 1922–27*
Blackburne or Bradshaw engines for this Bert Houlding-designed bike.

MATADOR *Germany 1925–26*
Own 369cc (22.5cu in) two-strokes.

MATCHLESS *England 1899–1966*
Matchless was unusual in the British motorcycle industry in that it operated outside the West Midlands, being established instead in Plumstead, South London. It was also one of the first marques in the business, H.H. Collier having been a maker of bicycles until joined in 1899 by his two eldest sons, Charlie and Harry, when he built his first motorized version. Matchless motorcycles would rarely show much innovation (with one or two notable exceptions) but built on commercial success by taking over no less than five rivals over the years, only for the whole construction to come to an undignified collapse in the mid-1960s. This was the first tangible sign that the British industry was heading for oblivion.

All this was in the future when the

ABOVE: Martinsyde built its own engines and survived for nearly seven years

BELOW: A 1939 Matchless 350cc (21cu in) G3

Colliers added a V-twin to their range in 1905, and which was to feature right up to 1939. It was powered by a bought-in engine, and indeed Matchless would not start making its own engines on a large scale until the 1920s. That first V-twin was quite advanced for its time, with leading-link forks and a type of swinging-arm rear suspension. Both Charlie and Harry were keen racers, and enjoyed some success riding it. Charlie actually won the first-ever Isle of Man TT race in 1907, his single-cylinder JAP-engined machine averaging 61.5km/h (38.22mph), not to mention fuel consumption of over 32km per litre (90mpg). Sibling rivalry was satisfied in 1909 when Harry won the TT, though Charlie snatched it back the following year. The two were also successful at Brooklands, riding Matchless bikes, of course.

Meanwhile, the road bikes were developing, with a three-speed hub gear added in 1912, which sadly meant dropping the innovative spring frame. Given the company's involvement in racing,there was also an adjustable engine pulley available to give two ranges and in theory six speeds, and belt tension was maintained by moving the rear wheel backwards. Also that year came the Colliers' first in-house engine, a four-stroke single of almost square 85.5mm x 85mm dimensions, though it lasted only a couple of years. Perhaps more successful were V-twins like the 8B, which now used an ioe V-twin built by MAG of Switzerland, and up-to-the-minute three-speed gearbox and enclosed chain-drive.

During World War I, Matchless did not supply motorcycles to the army, but went over to making munitions and aircraft parts.

Still, it did patriotically rename its V-twin the 'Victorious' in 1918. The civilian twins went back into production, now updated with electric lights and a return of the spring frame; but it wasn't until 1923 that a single rejoined the range. Once again, the engine came from outside, a 348cc (21cu in) sidevalve Blackburne, though the company's own 591cc (36cu in) single went into production the following year. It had been a while since there had been a sporting Matchless, and the 347cc overhead-camshaft single looked like it. Unfortunately, it only developed 13bhp, and although it remained in production for a short time, it was soon overshadowed by sharper ohc bikes from Velocette and others.

Undaunted, Matchless designed its own V-twin in 1925, a 990cc (60cu in) sidevalve that owed much to the 591cc single. Perhaps it was on more familiar ground here, for it was more of a success and stayed in production right up to 1939. It was followed by the company's smallest bike yet, a 250 sidevalve, the model R. At around this time H.H. Collier died, and shortly afterwards the family relinquished its control and Matchless went public. For 1927, the whole range was given a new look, with white-panelled fuel tanks in the new-style saddles, and meanwhile the range had grown to include 347 and 495cc (21 and 30cu in) ohv singles, followed by a 250cc (15cu in) ohv (the R3) in 1929.

All of these, however, were highly conventional bikes, though it has to be said that it was probably this full range of uncomplicated good-value machines that saw Matchless through the Depression. But the Silver Arrow of 1930 was

A 1958 Matchless 650cc (40cu in) G12

ABOVE: Ernie Dorsett's diesel-powered G80

ABOVE and BELOW: The 650cc (40cu in) G12 was Matchless' answer to BSA's A10 and Triumph's Thunderbird, but in comparison was not a success

anything but conventional. Quiet, well-mannered and with clean lines, the Silver Arrow was a narrow-angled V-twin of 398cc (24cu in). It continued Matchless' love of sprung rear frames but, as ever, the conservative public could not take to it. The same was true of the Silver Hawk which followed it a year later, a V4 along similar lines, with overhead camshaft and 593cc. Like the Arrow, it was much discussed, generating a good deal of interest but few sales.

So perhaps it was with a cynical eye on the fickle yet conservative public that Matchless turned its attention to sprucing up the singles in the latest style (sloping cylinders) and probably sold more bikes as a result. The company certainly hadn't suffered too much from the Arrow/Hawk failures, and was able to take over AJS in 1931. In 1935 it introduced the famous G range of singles (first named Clubman),

with either ohv or sidevalve engines, which grew into a range of 250, 350 and 500cc by 1938, the year Matchless also swallowed Sunbeam (only to sell it on to BSA a few years later). And it was the 350cc (21.4cu in) Matchless G3 that became the staple transport of the British Army from 1939. Two years later, in the midst of war, Matchless was to exhibit another one of its rare moments of innovation, with the Teledraulic telescopic fork. It wasn't a wholly new idea, but the Matchless version, with oil damping, was sufficiently new to be patented. (After the war, as all other manufactures rushed to build their own telescopics, it was clear that this time Matchless had got there first.)

Forks or not, Matchless' first post-war bikes were civilianized G singles, though the new G9 500cc (30.5cu in) twin appeared in 1948, complete with swinging-arm rear suspension with the company's own 'jampot' suspension units. A racing version, the G45, won the Senior Manx Grand Prix in 1952. That was the year Matchless (now Associated Motor Cycles, or AMC) bought up Norton and James. (Francis-Barnett had had already joined in 1947 and Brockhouse Engineering in 1959.) This combination of famous names, all of which would be concentrated at Plumstead, became renowned for badge engineering; in other words, whether you bought an AJS or Matchless made no difference as only the badge (and maybe the colour) could tell them apart.

In the spirit of the times, the twins grew in size and sporting aspirations with the 592cc (36cu in) G11, 646cc (39cu in)

G12 and the tuned G12 CSR. There was also a new 250cc single, the G2, while the G45 racer was dropped to make way for the G50 ohc single (really an enlarged AJS 7R). The 650 twins were supplemented by 750s in the early 1960s, but in keeping with strategy, the engines came from Norton. This sharing of parts actually made economic sense, and perhaps in different circumstances might have helped save AMC. As it was, the finances were in such a mess that a receiver was called in in 1966. Manganese Bronze Holdings stepped in to form the new Norton-Villiers Ltd., and for a couple of years produced Matchless-badged bikes that were really Nortons. Its real hopes, however, lay with the new Norton Commando, and with that Matchless finally died.

ABOVE and RIGHT: Matchless G80 500cc singles

The 592cc (36cu in) G11 was not a sporting bike, but it was a flexible tourer

MATRA *Hungary 1938–47*
98 or 198cc (6 or 12cu in) Sachs and Ardie two-strokes.

MAURER *Germany 1922–26*
Built its own two-strokes, including a 1.5hp clip-on, 247cc (15cu in) vertical twin, and 494cc (30cu in) water-cooled flat twin.

MAUSER *Germany 1924–32*
The most car-like bike ever, the Einspurauto used a car-type body and chassis, with two retractable outrigger wheels to keep it upright when stationary. At 289kg (638lb) it was rather heavy for its 10bhp, 510cc (31cu in) sv single. Mauser didn't sell many, though French firm Monotrace made them under licence.

MAVISA *Spain 1957–60*
Upmarket two-stroke twin with shaft-drive.

MAWI *Germany 1923–30*
Used bought-in two-stroke DKW and four-stroke JAP engines to 546cc (33cu in).

MAX *Germany 1924–25*
Produced a 180cc (11cu in) two-stroke and 446cc (27cu in) sv single, both in-house.

MAX *France 1927–30*
Used a variety of bought-in engines to 496cc (30cu in).

MAXIM *England 1919–21*
Fitted 318cc (19.4cu in) Dalm single-cylinder two-strokes.

MAXIMA *Italy 1920–25*
Built its own big flat twins of 690/747cc (42/46cu in).

MAZZUCHELLI *Italy 1925–28*
Imported the 198cc (12cu in) Alba engine to power its simple machine.

MB *Czechoslovakia 1927–28*
A rotary-valve 498cc (30cu in) single, in which the valve controlled both inlet and exhaust.

MB *U.S.A. 1916–20*
Advanced for its time, it was a 746cc (45.5cu in) vertical-twin with shaft-drive.

MBM *Italy 1974–81*
Minarelli-engined mopeds.

MCB *Sweden 1960–75*
The Monark Crescent Bolagen group, the result of Monark's takeover of other Swedish makes.

MCC *England 1903–c.1910*
Used De Dion, Minerva and other engines, and built its own under licence from Minerva.

McEVOY *England 1926–29*
Started with a Villiers-engined lightweight, then used Blackburne and JAP engines plus Anzani big V-twins. Designer George Patchett (ex-Brough-Superior, pre-Jawa) produced a prototype 346cc (21cu in) three-valve ohc single and 498cc (30cu in) in-line four.

McKECHNIE *England 1922*
688cc (42cu in) Coventry-Victor flat twin, with rear suspension.

McKENZIE *England 1921–25*
196cc (12cu in) two-strokes in conventional or step-through frames.

MDS *Italy 1955–60*
Modern unit-construction four-stroke singles of 65–80cc (4–5cu in).

MEAD *England 1911–16*
Wide range of machines, with engines from Precision, JAP and Premier.

MEGOLA *Germany 1921–25*
Perhaps the oddest motorcycle ever to reach production, the Megola mounted a five-cylinder radial engine (640cc/39cu in) within the front wheel. No clutch, no gears, and the only way to alter the direct-drive ratio was to purchase a different sized wheel. There was no room in the front wheel for a brake, so the maker fitted two to the rear. It could top 113km/h (70mph) on the road (racers managed 137km/h/85mph) and some had rear suspension. The low centre of gravity gave good handling, and Megola actually sold nearly 200 of them.

MEGURO *Japan 1937–64*
Mainly English-influenced singles up to 498cc (30cu in) and a copy of the BSA A10 twin from 1961. Taken over by Kawasaki late in its life.

MEIHATSU *Japan 1953–61*
Kawasaki subsidiary, with two-strokes up to 248cc (15cu in).

MEISTER *Germany 1951–56*
All two-stroke lightweights and mopeds of 49–198cc (3–12cu in).

MEMINI *Italy 1946–47*
Own 173cc (11cu in) two-stroke.

MENON *Italy 1930–32*
Small tourers, with 174 and 198cc (11 and 12cu in) sv singles.

MENOS *Germany 1922–23*
Almost identical to the Aristos, with the same water-cooled 614cc (37.5cu in) flat twin.

MERAY *Hungary 1921–44*
A wide variety of bought-in engines were used by this leading Hungarian company, with its own singles from 1936.

MERCIER *France 1950–62*
Used engines from Lafalette, Villiers and Ydral.

MERCO *Germany 1922–24*
Own 148cc (9cu in) three-port two-strokes.

MERCURY *England 1956–58*
Lightweights and scooters up to 98cc (6cu in).

MERKEL *U.S.A. 1901–22*
Built own singles and V-twins up to 986cc (60cu in) before takeover by Indian.

MERLI *Italy 1929–31*
Used 173cc (11cu in) Train two-strokes.

MERLONGHI *Italy 1927–30*
132cc (8cu in) two-stroke, two-speed machines.

METEOR *Czechoslovakia 1909–26*
211cc (13cu in) clip-ons, then utility two-stroke lightweights.

METEOR *Germany 1924–26*
Used a 172cc (10.5cu in) two-stroke, possibly imported from Thumann of France.

METEORA *Italy 1953–66*
Used various bought-in engines for these lightweights, which included a motocross bike.

METRO *England 1912–19*
269cc (16cu in) two-stroke with two- or three-speed gearbox.

Sales brochure for the Meguro range

MEYBEIN *Germany 1922–26*
Bike with low-slung frame and 119/142cc (7/9cu in) DKW power.

MEYBRA *Germany 1923–25*
Used own 168cc (10cu in) two-stroke.

MEZO *Austria 1923–26*
Used imported Villiers and JAP engines for a limited production run.

MF *Germany 1922–25*
First used BMW's early flat twin, later Blackburne singles to 497cc (30cu in).

MFB *Germany 1923–24*
Wooden frames distinguished MFB from the rest, with 198cc (12cu in) Nabob or 293cc (18cu in) JAP units.

MGC *France 1927–29*
Had a light alloy frame which incoporated the fuel tank and was JAP or Chaise-powered.

MGF *Italy 1921–25*
Used bought-in Bekamo engines, but also made its own and sold them to others.

MG/TAURUS *Italy 1926–50*
Founded by Vittorio Guerzoni, who first used 173cc (11cu in) Train engines before building his own 248/496cc (15/30cu in) ohv, and later ohc singles. From 1933 also sold under the Taurus name, and when taken over by the Bergamini brothers after the war they sold the 250/500cc (15/30.5cu in) machines under the Centaurus name.

MIAMI *U.S.A. 1905–23*
Connected with Merkel, it also built its own 298cc (18cu in) sv singles.

MICHAELSON *U.S.A. 1910–15*
Advanced singles and V-twins with ohv, leaf-sprung forks and chain-drive.

MIDGET-BICAR *U.S.A. 1908–1909*
A welded and riveted steel frame was powered by a big V-twin – not a success.

MIELE *Germany 1933–62*
Began fitting Sachs engines to its bicycles, and after 1945 remained loyal to Sachs to power its mopeds and lightweights.

MIGNON *Italy 1923–32*
123cc (7.5cu in) clip-ons led to a 246cc (15cu in) sv twin, then a 498cc (30cu in) single with either ohv or ohc.

MILANI *Italy 1970–81*
Built mopeds and off-road bikes, Minarelli-powered. Many were exported to the U.S.A.

MILITAIRE *U.S.A. 1911–17*
One of the American in-line fours, though at 1306cc (80cu in) it was one of the biggest. It had a one-piece frame, three-speed plus reverse gearbox and leaf-sprung rear-end. The Militaire was built by no less than eight companies in its short history.

MILLER *U.S.A. c.1903*
Over the years there were numerous small motorcycle companies which quickly came and went during the industry's formative years. This is one of them and there is little evidence of its existence beyond yellowing advertisements in old cycling magazines.

MILLER-BALSAMO *Italy 1921–59*
First used 123cc (7.5cu in) two-strokes, but

ABOVE and RIGHT: *The Miller was an American pioneer*

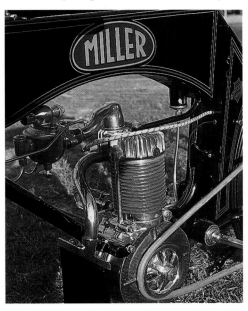

was soon building four-valve Python singles under licence. Later there was a 98cc (6cu in) Sachs-engined lightweight and fully-enclosed 198cc (12cu in) bike. Concentrated on two-strokes after 1945, apart from slightly updated pre-war singles and an ohc 169cc (10cu in) single.

MILLIONMOBILE *England c.1902*
1.5hp engine in a cycle frame.

MIMOA *Germany 1924*
Used the Julius Löwy-designed two-stroke that would run on crude oil.

MINERVA *Belgium 1900–09*
Prolific engine maker which sold its power units (and the licences to make them) all over the world, but also made complete bikes up to 1909. There was a motorized cycle in 1900, culminating in a 580cc (35cu in) V-twin by 1909.

MINETTI *Italy 1924–1927*
124cc (8cu in) three-port two-stroke.

MINEUR *Belgium 1924–28*
Paul Mineur built his own 348/496cc (21/30cu in) sv singles, as well as using JAP, Bradshaw, MAG and Sarolea units.

MINISCOOT *France 1960–62*
A folding 74cc (4.5cu in) two-stroke mini-scooter.

MINNEAPOLIS *U.S.A. 1908–15*
Used various V-twins as well as its own unit-construction sv single. It had early chain-drive and (according to one source) telescopic forks.

MINSK *Russia 1954–*
Another version of the much-copied DKW 125, this one updated over the years. Five million have been sold.

MIRANDA *Germany 1951–54*
Scooter with 173cc (11cu in) Sachs or 198cc (12cu in) Küchen power.

MISTRAL *France 1902–early 1960s*
Started with a 1.75hp bike, and remained with lightweights up to 247cc (15cu in) after World War II. Also supplied moped engines to others.

MITCHELL *U.S.A. 1901–c.1906*
345cc (21cu in) single with rearward-facing cylinder.

MI-VAL *Italy 1950–66*
123cc (7.5cu in) two-stroke followed by four-strokes up to 199cc (12cu in).

MIYATA *Japan 1909–64*
One of the few pre-war Japanese makes offering 123cc (7.5cu in) two-stroke, mid-sized four-stroke singles, and 496cc (30cu in) vertical twins.

MJ *Germany 1924–25*
Its own 249cc (15cu in) two-stroke never reached full production, but MJ supplied flat twins to other manufacturers.

MJS *Germany 1924–25*
Built its own 245cc (15cu in) three-port two-strokes.

MM *U.S.A. 1905–c.1914*
Used a variety of bought-in engines from Thomas, Marsh, Royal, Holley and Pope.

MM *Italy 1924–64*
Concentrated on racers until producing its first road bikes in the 1930s. They were ohv and sv singles up to 498cc (30cu in), but were still heavily biased towards racing. One of the founders was Alfonso Morini who left in 1937 to set up his own firm. After 1945, MM based its 350 and 500cc (21 and 30.5cu in) singles on pre-war designs, though there was also a new ohc 250. Also made a 125cc (8cu in) two-stroke in its final years.

M&M *England 1914*
Step-through frame with 169cc (10cu in) Villiers engine.

MMM *Germany 1925–27*
148cc (9cu in) two-stroke machines.

MOCHET *France 1950–55*
149cc (9cu in) Ydral-powered lightweights.

MOFA *Germany 1920–25*
Clip-ons of 70 and 148cc (4.3 and 9cu in).

MOHAWK *England 1903–25*
Pioneered with 2.5/3hp engines, then withdrew until the 1920s to have another attempt at using a wide range of bought-in engines, including a 346cc (21cu in) JAP.

MOLARONI *Italy 1921–27*
Built its own 269cc (16cu in) two-stroke and 596cc (36cu in) flat twin (which had automatic lubrication). On one model, also used the Blackburne 348cc (21cu in) single.

MOLTENI *Italy 1925–27*
Forward-thinking use of aluminium alloy for the frame, fork and chain cases and with Bradshaw or MAG power. Not a success.

MONACO-BAUDO *Italy 1926–28*
Own unit-construction single of 496cc (30cu in), though later used bought-in JAP and Blackburne engines.

MONARCH *U.S.A. 1912–25*
Another North American factory which produced 496cc (30cu in) singles and 990cc (60cu in) V-twins with its own ioe engines in sprung frames.

MONARCH *England 1919–21*
A cheaper version of the Excelsior, Villiers-powered.

MONARCH *Japan 1955–62*
Ohv singles of 346/496cc (21/30cu in), with Norton influence.

MONARK *Sweden 1927–75*
Actually built its first bike in 1913, but the Monark name was not used until 1927 on a range of Blackburne-engined singles to 600cc (37cu in). Built a 98cc (6cu in) Ilo-powered lightweight from 1936, and Albin 500cc four-strokes for the Swedish army during World War II. Concentrated largely on Ilo-engined lightweights of 50–250cc.

The Montesa was an important marque for Spain

(3–15cu in) and some 500cc machines with British parts after the war until production ceased in 1975.

MONFORT *Spain 1957–59*
123/197cc (7.5/12cu in) Hispano-Villiers two-strokes.

MONOPOLE *England 1911–28*
Used Abingdon, JAP or Villiers engines to 680cc (41.5cu in).

MONOTRACE *France 1926–28*
Licence-built version of the German Mauser car-like bike.

MONTEROSA *Italy 1954–58*
Made 49cc (3cu in) mopeds only.

MONTESA *Spain 1945–*
Spain's first major marque, the company was founded by Francesco Bulto and Pedro Permanyer and has always built its own two-strokes. Started with a 98cc (6cu in) lightweight, which was soon followed by a 125cc (8cu in). Montesa also found its niche in off-road competition, and was a dominant force there for many years. Bulto left in 1958 to set up Bultaco, but 1962 saw the unveiling of the Impala, with an all-new 175cc (11cu in) engine. A 250cc (15cu in) and racing versions followed. Alongside all of this, Montesa continued to make road-going two-strokes of up to 349cc (21cu in). Sales collapsed at the end of the 1970s, but even the successful relaunch of the Impala in 1981 couldn't prevent a Honda takeover. Montesa still makes its own Cota trials bike, and assembles small Hondas.

MONTGOMERY *England 1902–39*
Always used bought-in engines, from Villiers to Anzani, though from the mid-

1930s only mid-sized JAP singles were used, notably in the sporting Greyhound model. Also built frames for Brough-Superior and P&P.

MONTLHÉRY *Austria 1926–28*
A 346cc (21cu in) JAP-powered machine.

MONVISO *Italy 1951–56*
All bikes utilized Sachs engines of 98–173cc (6–11cu in).

MOONBEAM *England 1920–21*
Romantic name for a 296cc (18cu in) Villiers-powered utility.

MORETTI *Italy 1934–52*
Limited production, but with engines from Ladetto, DKW and JAP as well as ohc units after 1945.

MORRIS *England 1902–05*
Lord Nuffield (William Morris) built motorcycles before achieving a fortune and knighthood from producing cars. Used 2.75hp De Dion or MMC engines.

MORRIS *England 1913–22*
Made 247cc (15cu in) three-port two-strokes. No connection with the above.

MORRIS-WARNE *England 1922*
A 248cc (15cu in) two-stroke, oddly offered with a vertical or horizontal cylinder.

MORS (SPEED) *France 1951–56*
Scooters from 60cc to 124cc (4 to 8cu in), produced in part of the original Mors car factory.

MORSE-BEAUREGARD *U.S.A. 1912–17*
Advanced unit-construction in-line twin, with shaft-drive.

MORTON-ADAM *England 1923–24*
Built 292cc (18cu in) two-strokes, and 248/348cc (15/21cu in) ohc singles designed by Harry Sidney.

MOSER *Switzerland 1905–35*
Built a complete range of bikes from 123–598cc (7.5–36.5cu in), and supplied ready-made power units to many rival factories. Most of these were ohv singles, especially the 123/173cc (7.5/11cu in) units.

MOSER *Austria 1953–54*
Used a 98cc (6cu in) Rotax engine, and was the forerunner of KTM.

MOTAG *Germany 1923–24*
An interesting machine, its frame was made of electron and there was the option of air- or water-cooling for its vertical twins of 514, 642 and 804cc (31.4, 39 and 49cu in).

MOTA-WIESEL *Germany 1948–52*
Small-wheeled scooter of 74–98cc (4.5-6cu in).

MOTOBÉCANE (MBK) *France 1923–*
Long-lived French factory, which changed its name to MBK in 1984 and has recently been taken over by Yamaha. Began with low-cost 172cc (10.5cu in) belt-driven two-strokes which were soon joined by one of 308cc (19cu in). Also introduced 'Moto Confort', under which name Motobécanes were also sold. It made four-stroke singles

of 172–498cc (10.5–30cu in) in the twenties and thirties, and in-line ohc fours (biggest was 749cc/46cu in) with shaft-drive. Smaller ohv singles remained in production until 1960. Most popular post-war product was the 49cc (3cu in) Mobylette, though motorcycle production ceased in 1964 only to restart five years later. There was a 125 two-stroke and 350 triple in the 1970s, but the company has really concentrated on mopeds. The Yamaha takeover means that MBK will make Yamaha mopeds for Europe bearing either badge.

MOTOBI *Italy 1950–80*
Giovanni Benelli left the family firm to set up MotoBi, whose trademark was the horizontal-cylinder, egg-shaped power unit. Began with 98cc (6cu in) two-strokes, progressing to 248cc (15cu in) and from 1956 produced 123/172cc (7.5/10.5cu in) four-strokes. MotoBi was re-absorbed by Benelli in 1962 when Giuseppe Benelli died, and after a while the bikes became rebadged Benellis, the MotoBi tradename being used up to 1980.

MOTOBIC *Spain 1949–65*
Produced mopeds and a 122cc (7.5cu in) lightweight and later made the Agrati Capri scooter under licence.

MOTOBIMM *Italy 1969–71*
Limited production of Minarelli-powered 49cc (3cu in) motocross and trials bikes.

MOTOBLOC *France 1948–54*
Produced mopeds, the 65cc (4cu in) Sulky scooter and lightweight motorcycles up to 248cc (15cu in), the latter with two-stroke or AMC four-stroke singles.

The 1949 Motoleggera: Moto Guzzi later had to abandon its enthusiast machines for a while

Moto Guzzi Falcone

MOTO-BORGO *Italy 1906–26*
Built big singles in the early days up to 827cc (50.5cu in), but developed a 990cc (60cu in) V-twin during World War I. Later produced a unit-construction 477cc (29cu in) V-twin, which could be had with four-valve heads. The Borgo brothers stopped making motorcyles in 1926 to concentrate on piston-making.

MOTOCLETTE *Switzerland 1904–15*
Fitted with Zedel and Moser engines.

MOTO GELIS *Argentina c.1955–62*
Licence-built 125cc (8cu in) Sachs engines, with other parts from Italy.

MOTO GUZZI *Italy 1921–*
Soichiro Honda, Michio Suzuki, Bill Harley and the Davidson brothers – many

motorcycle companies still bear the names of their original founders, and Moto Guzzi is no exception. As World War I came to its final stages, Carlo Guzzi had played his part in Italy's new Air Corps, but his real love was motorcycles. He was an instinctive designer and given to producing innovative ideas. However, there was one small flaw in the Guzzi dream of a new career in motorcycling – he came from a poor Milanese family and there was no money.

It is at this point that the origins of Moto Guzzi begin to sound like a fairy tale. Among Carlo's friends were two well-heeled young flying officers, Giorgio Parodi and Giovanni Ravelli, both of whom shared his fascination with bikes. Between them it was agreed that Guzzi should design a new world beater, Parodi would find the money

to build it, and Ravelli would ride the bike to victory on the race tracks. Sadly, Ravelli was killed in a flying accident only days after the war ended, and it is said that Moto Guzzi's flying eagle badge was a tribute to a potential champion. Undaunted, the other two pressed on, Parodi hoping to persuade his father to fund the building of the first prototype. Parodi Snr. was suitably impressed, and he did.

Completed in 1920, that first bike bristled with innovative features: unit-construction, oversquare bore/stroke, four valves per cylinder (with ohc) and gear primary-drive. It also established an engine layout which was to remain with Moto Guzzi for many years, in which the single 498cc (30cu in) cylinder was laid horizontally, with an external flywheel. That

flywheel (the 'bacon slicer') was eventually enclosed, but the basic layout of an air-cooled, horizontal four-stroke single, in unit with the gearbox, would still be in production in the mid-1970s. The rest of the machine was more conventional, with a three-speed hand-change gearbox, girder front forks and rear brake only. As a matter of fact, when the realities of production and sales made themselves felt, Guzzi's advanced prototype had to be somewhat diluted and the four-valve overhead-cam layout was abandoned for an overhead inlet/side-exhaust system (common at the time) with just two valves.

But although Guzzi had to compromise on his original vision, the racing success did come, and with it the means to build more exotic machinery. In only its second event, the new 'Moto Guzzi' (it was Parodi, incidentally, who suggested the name) won the Targa Florio race, ridden by Gino Finzi. Over the next couple of years, more race wins in Italy encouraged Guzzi to resurrect his four-valve design, which rewarded him by winning the German Grand Prix in 1924. A smaller 249cc (15cu in) version followed, which was only denied a debut second place at the Isle of Man TT by disqualification, allegedly because the wrong make of spark plug had been used. Still, Moto Guzzi had its revenge and went on to win both Junior and Senior TTs in the same year, both of them ridden by Stanley Woods.

Falcone Flies
During the war, of course, Moto Guzzi carried on building its horizontal singles for the military, though only 8,000 were delivered in four years. But in the late

1940s, Italy needed cheap, basic transport rather than machines for enthusiasts like the big singles. So Moto Guzzi, like just about every other Italian manufacturer at the time, turned its attention to small two-strokes. The 65 Guzzino (Little Guzzi) was the result, a 64cc (3.9cu in) single in a mild state of tune (just 2bhp at 5,000rpm), which meant a top speed of little more than 48km/h (30mph), but up to 71km per litre (200mpg)! It was a great success, with 200,000 sold before the Guzzino was replaced by the Cardellino in 1954. Telescopic forks and a larger 73cc (4.5cu in) version followed, as well as the 98cc (6cu in) Zigolo, with its pressed steel frame and 19-inch wheels. But unusually, Guzzi made small four-strokes as well.

The 160cc (9.8cu in) Galletto was unveiled in 1950, and was a large-wheeled scooter which sold very well, benefiting from capacity increases to 174 and 192cc (10.6 and 11.7cu in) over the years: it survived until 1966. A more exotic lightweight was the 175cc overhead-cam Lodolo (launched 1956), of which there were later 235 and 250 versions, not to mention the works

ISDT bikes. The Stornello, meanwhile, was a cheaper ohv roadster, which started off in 1960 as a 125, growing to 160cc in 1967.

But Moto Guzzi had not forgotten its roots, and continued to offer big 'flat' singles after the war. Most famous was the Falcone of 1950, which was actually no more nor less than a mild update of the pre-war big single. The frame was new and the electrics were uprated, but the Falcone was substantially the same as the 1938 GTW. Far from being outdated, however, it was still fast enough (tuned Falcones could exceed 161km/h/100mph) to excel in long-distance road racing. In Grand Prix too, the 350cc (21cu in) racer (thanks in part to Scotsman Fergus Anderson) retained the World Championship right up to 1957. And the customers loved the traditional Guzzi big single, so much so that the company simply updated it in 1963 and 1969, and it went on selling to private buyers as well as to the usual police and military markets. But back in the 1950s, Moto Guzzi realized that the single could not go on dominating world-class racing forever, and its answer was the astonishing V8 of 1956. Just like that very first prototype, the 500cc (30.5cu in) V8 racer was advanced for its day, with liquid-cooling, twin overhead camshafts and a rev limit of 12,000rpm. It had tremendous speed and great promise, but Guzzi pulled out of racing in 1957. So that was that.

The V-twin is Born
Apart from all the racing success (and even after the withdrawal from track racing, ISDT medals and speed records came Moto Guzzi's way), much of the company's business which earned it its living came

The post-1950 Falcone was an update of the pre-war single

ABOVE: Moto Guzzi 350cc (21cu in)

from selling flat singles to the Italian police and army. But by the early 1960s, even these uniformed customers were looking for more power and the answer was to come from an unusual quarter. In the late 1950s, the army itself had outlined the need for a type of mini-tractor, and Moto Guzzi had duly come up with a 90-degree overhead-valve V-twin. Of 754cc (46cu in), it was suitably tractor-like. However, it was also to be the basis of Guzzi's fortunes for the next three decades.

History does not record who it was at Moto Guzzi who suggested adapting the tractor engine for a tough, utilitarian motorcycle, but that's what was done. Capacity was reduced to 703cc (43cu in),

and the engine was mated to a car-type dry clutch, four-speed gearbox and shaft-drive. Just like the original flat single, this basic layout was to stay with Moto Guzzi for a long time (and at the time of writing, still does). The V7, submitted for governmental approval in early 1965, looked what it was – big, heavy and solid rather than stylish. Despite its lumpy looks, the V7 got an enthusiastic reception when unveiled at the Milan Show at the end of the year. Here was a 161km/h (100mph) tourer that promised simple maintenance and long life, and there was nothing else quite like it. Apart from Harley-Davidsons, V-twins had virtually disappeared, and at the time no one else (BMW excepted) offered shaft-drive.

BELOW: The S3 was precursor to Le Mans

BELOW: The 1974 Moto Guzzi Sahara, the last of the 500 singles

The V50, seen here in traffic-police form, was a new series of smaller V-twins

Although the first civilian V7s did not reach customers until 1967, development for the civilian market continued rapidly thereafter. A V7 Special (now 757cc, and with power up to 45bhp) sold in America in 1969 as the Ambassador, while in 1971 came variations on a theme that sparked off three distinct models: another capacity increase produced the 850GT (844cc/51.5cu in) which took care of the touring market; the GT California was in the American mould (screen, panniers, high and wide bars), and a California has featured in the Guzzi range ever since. The V7 Sport was the first in a long line of sporting Guzzi V-twins and while the first two were close developments of the original V7, the Sport was one step further

ABOVE and BELOW: Sales brochure for the Moto Guzzi V50 Monza. The 'small' V-twin eventually grew to 750cc

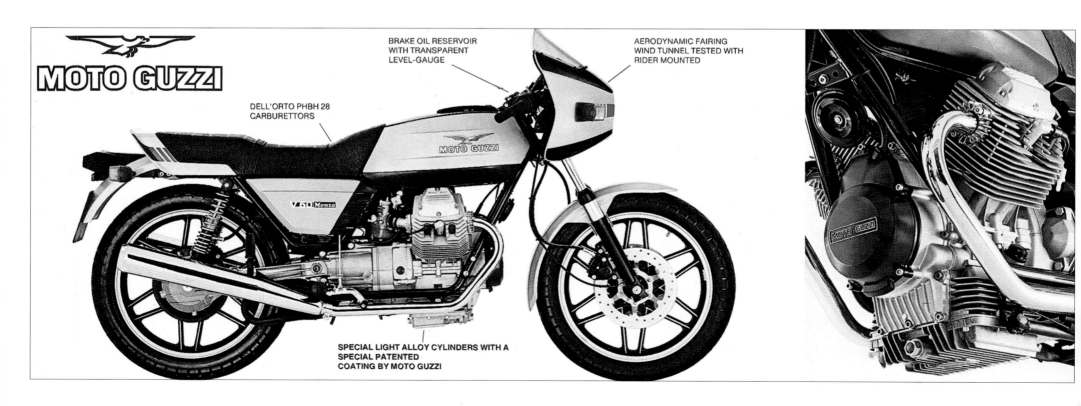

BRAKE OIL RESERVOIR WITH TRANSPARENT LEVEL-GAUGE

AERODYNAMIC FAIRING WIND TUNNEL TESTED WITH RIDER MOUNTED

DELL'ORTO PHBH 28 CARBURETTORS

SPECIAL LIGHT ALLOY CYLINDERS WITH A SPECIAL PATENTED COATING BY MOTO GUZZI

ABOVE and BELOW: The V7 Sport was the first development of the touring V7

on. New design head, Lino Tonti, transformed the chassis by lowering it (the trick was replacing the high-mounted dynamo with an alternator on the end of the crank), which changed the whole character of the machine. Higher compression, bigger carburettors and more sporting cam profiles added up to 52bhp at 6,300rpm, while Tonti made sure to keep the Sport's capacity below 750cc (actually 749cc) to keep it eligible for 750 racing. This new style of Guzzi V-twin went on sale in 1972.

The V7 Sport became a 750S in 1974,

but a real leap forward came the following year with the Le Mans. As well as a new name, it used a tuned version of the 844cc touring twin, now with 10.2:1 compression, bigger than ever 36mm Dell'Orto carburettors, larger valves and 71bhp, enough for a top speed of 200km/h (124mph). A factory race kit liberated still more power, and the Le Mans went on to several racing victories. It was heartening that with the same gearing as the tourers, the Le Mans would lope along at high speeds in a very relaxed manner, providing a true alternative to the Japanese four-cylinder sportsbikes. Unfortunately, it also became famous for poor finish, a recurring Moto Guzzi problem. There were no fundamental changes to the Le Mans in the next few years, though it did get a little softer as tougher noise regulations came into force. A 948cc (58cu in) Le Mans arrived in 1984, which produced 86bhp and a claimed 225km/h (140mph), as well as Moto Guzzi's infamous experimentation with 16-inch front wheels. The latter was an attempt to ape Japanese sportsbikes, but were fundamentally unsuited to the heavier, long-wheelbased Guzzi. They were quickly dropped, and the Le Mans continued with an 18-inch wheel up to 1991

Variations on a Theme
Meanwhile, the 850GT and California had acquired the lower, alternator-equipped engine, and were joined by the automatic transmission V1000 Convert. The latter had a clutch, but this was only needed for swapping ratios in the two-speed gearbox and a Sachs torque converter took care of stopping and starting. It was an interesting idea, but not a commercial success. Honda

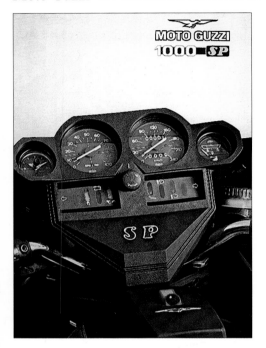

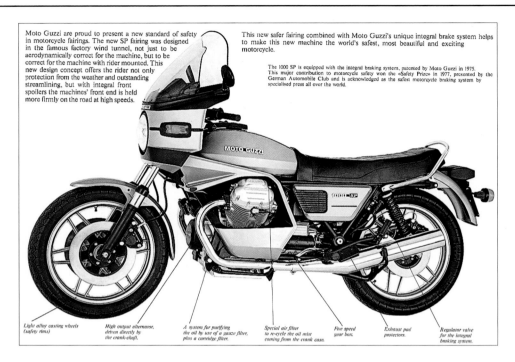

Moto Guzzi are proud to present a new standard of safety in motorcycle fairings. The new SP fairing was designed in the famous factory wind tunnel, not just to be aerodynamically correct for the machine, but to be correct for the machine with rider mounted. This new design concept offers the rider not only protection from the weather and outstanding streamlining, but with integral front spoilers the machines' front end is held more firmly on the road at high speeds.

This new safer fairing combined with Moto Guzzi's unique integral brake system helps to make this new machine the world's safest, most beautiful and exciting motorcycle.

The 1000 SP is equipped with the integral braking system, patented by Moto Guzzi in 1975. This major contribution to motorcycle safety won the «Safety Prize» in 1977, presented by the German Automobile Club and is acknowledged as the safest motorcycle braking system by specialised press all over the world.

Light alloy casting wheels (safety rims). High output alternator, driven directly by the crank-shaft. A system for purifying the oil by use of a gauze filter, plus a cartridge filter. Special air filter to re-cycle the oil mist coming from the crank case. Five speed gear box. Exhaust pad protectors. Regulator valve for the integral braking system.

ABOVE: The 1000SP – Moto Guzzi's tilt at the BMW market

BELOW: The Galletto scooter had a single-sided swinging arm

found the same thing when attempting to sell its 400cc (24cu in) twin and 750cc (46cu in) Hondamatics at about the same time. More promising was the SP, or Spada, unveiled in 1977, which used the 949cc twin with a conventional five-speed gearbox and designed-in fairing. The fairing was a two-piece affair, with the top half handlebar-mounted, and the whole was allegedly designed in Moto Guzzi's own wind tunnel at the Mandello del Lario factory. With decent weather protection, it certainly made the most of the Guzzi V-twin's long-legged nature, and cost less than a BMW; but again, the finish was below par and the SP failed to take a big chunk out of BMW's market. An SPIII (from 1984) used a conventional one-piece, frame-mounted fairing.

The 1980s was also the decade when retro bikes first appeared, with no fairing and vaguely 1970s styling with modern underpinnings. Moto Guzzi's first offering was the 1000S, with the latest version of the 948cc V-twin, but with styling which echoed that of the 750S. Similarly, the Mille GT of 1989 reintroduced the basic roadster Guzzi, albeit with the biggest engine. Another variant on the big V-twin theme was the Quota, which with its vaguely off-road styling was part of the 'adventure-tourer' sector, made popular with bikes like the Cagiva Elefant and Honda Africa Twin. The Quota followed a familiar formula, using a roadster engine (the 949cc twin) with its own chassis, longer travel suspension and dual-purpose tyres. Like most bikes of its type, though,

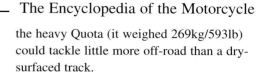

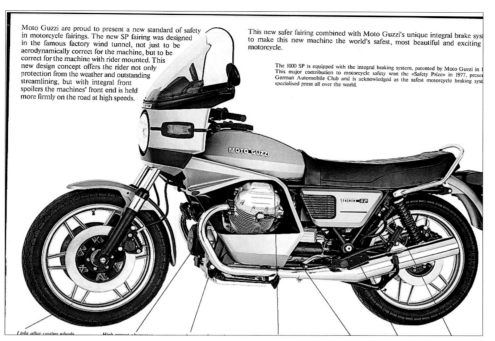

Moto Guzzi are proud to present a new standard of safety in motorcycle fairings. The new SP fairing was designed in the famous factory wind tunnel, not just to be aerodynamically correct for the machine, but to be correct for the machine with rider mounted. This new design concept offers the rider not only protection from the weather and outstanding streamlining, but with integral front spoilers the machines' front end is held more firmly on the road at high speeds.

This new safer fairing combined with Moto Guzzi's unique integral brake sys to make this new machine the world's safest, most beautiful and exciting motorcycle.

The 1000 SP is equipped with the integral braking system, patented by Moto Guzzi in This major contribution to motorcycle safety won the «Safety Prize» in 1977, prese German Automobile Club and is acknowledged as the safest motorcycle braking syst specialised press all over the world.

the heavy Quota (it weighed 269kg/593lb) could tackle little more off-road than a dry-surfaced track.

Moto Guzzi's smaller trail bikes were better liked, however, especially the V35 TT, which was lighter and handier but still had enough torque for riding off-road. Together with the similar-looking V65 TT, it was restyled as the NTX in 1987, and had another makeover in the early nineties. Incidentally, those smaller V-twins had been part of the Moto Guzzi range for some time. Their origins lay in the early 1970s when Argentinian-born industrialist Alejandro de Tomaso took over Moto Guzzi (not to mention Benelli) and determined to raise production, cut costs and build the Italian industry back up again. Early attempts to attach Moto Guzzi badges to the small two- and four-stroke Benellis met with

BELOW: The V10 Centauro Sport filled the gap between California and the four-valved sports Guzzis

ABOVE: The late-edition Le Mans was replaced by the four-valved Daytona (BELOW)

limited success, so De Tomaso decided to do it properly, authorizing chief designer Lino Tonti to build a smaller version of the classic big V-twin.

Tonti succeeded in no uncertain terms, as the V35 (346cc/21cu in) and V50 (490cc/30cu in), unveiled in September 1976, were real big Guzzis in miniature. They had the same transverse air-cooled pushrod V-twin layout, with shaft-drive and Guzzi's linked braking system. The V50 in particular won a lot of friends; compared with the rival Honda CX500, it was lighter and handled very well with about the same performance, and it was even cheaper! Sadly, the small twins suffered from quality problems which weren't really addressed until the much-improved V50III of 1980. There was still a gap in the Guzzi range, filled first by V65, then V75 developments of the small twin. And as well as the trail bikes, there were cruisers with various engine sizes. Four-valve versions of the roadsters followed in 1984, but these suffered from the now familiar teething troubles. Overall though, the De Tomaso-inspired mini-Guzzis did much to bolster the company's fortunes, and developments remain in the line-up to this day.

Dr. John's Magic

But perhaps more significant for Moto Guzzi in the 1990s has been the arrival of the overhead-camshaft V-twin – the Daytona. It came about largely thanks to one John Wittner, an American who had had great success in endurance racing with his own Guzzi-powered racer. So successful was he that Alejandro De Tomaso gave the former dentist from Philadelphia a prototype eight-valve ohc twin that had been designed at the factory. In fairy-tale fashion, the resultant race bike was third in its debut race (the 1988 Daytona Twins) and more podium positions followed that year. As a result, Wittner (or 'Dr. John' as he became known, in deference to his medical background) was invited to Italy to develop a road-going version of the Daytona.

This he did, and the new Daytona made its debut for customers at the 1991 Milan Show. It was a success. The new engine, with its belt-driven overhead cams and Weber-Marelli fuel injection, produced 100bhp (more than any previous road-going Moto Guzzi). Better still for the enthusiasts, its well-finned, air-cooled cylinders on proud display below the half-fairing could not be mistaken for anything else – this was not a Guzzi made bland by the modern world. So well received was the Daytona that the company soon came up with a cheaper alternative in the 1100 Sport (all the big twins had since grown to 1100cc/67cu in) which married Daytona styling with the older pushrod V-twin. At the time, the motorcycle market was beginning to fragment into niches, and it made sense to produce a number of variations on the same theme. The Centauro was one result of this, using the Daytona's fuel-injected twin in a decidedly retro motorcycle whose styling owed little to previous Moto Guzzis, or indeed anything else. Still a big, heavy motorcycle with shaft-drive, but now with a lot of power that was arguably best used in a straight line, journalist Alan Cathcart described the Centauro as 'a two-wheeled AC Cobra', which was about right.

But the world was moving on, and Moto Guzzi knew that ever-tighter noise and emission regulations meant it couldn't remain with an air-cooled engine for ever. Its answer was an all-new 75-degree V-twin whose basic layout (though not a running engine) was shown to the press in the summer of 1998. Financial backing from the American Tamarix Investment Bank had given the project a further boost, and Moto Guzzi announced that the liquid-cooled eight-valve dohc V-twin – its first all-new engine for 20 years – would power a complete range of bikes, in sizes ranging from 850cc to 1200cc (52 to 73cu in). The 998cc (61cu in) prototype was projected to produce 170bhp at the rear wheel in race form (an assault on World Superbike racing was part of the plan) with 135bhp at 11,000rpm for the road. And it would retain that unique Moto Guzzi feature, being mounted transversely in the frame, which would make it more compact than the Ducati-inspired rivals.

However, as time went on it became clear that all was not well. Moto Guzzi's recently-appointed chief executive, Oscar Cecchinato, had ambitious plans to triple production and take Moto Guzzi back into mass-production and this, in turn, dictated a move from the lakeside Mandello del Lario factory (historic, evocative, but cramped). A new factory was lined up but, at what seemed like the eleventh hour, there was a revolt. Faced with a four-hour commute to the new factory, the workforce voted against moving, while upper management threatened mass resignation if the now unpopular Cecchinato refused to leave. He was duly dismissed, and at the time of writing, Moto Guzzi was set to stay at Mandello; mass-production plans had been pruned but development of the all-new V-twin would continue. Life was never dull at Moto Guzzi.

The Ambassador V7, Moto Guzzi's first V-twin, used an engine derived from a military mini-tractor